The Insider's Guide to Ecommerce

440 business insights for the ambitious online retailer

Chris Barling

The Insider's Guide to Ecommerce:
440 business insights for the ambitious online retailer
By Chris Barling

January 2013: First Edition.

ISBN 978-0-9575319-0-1

Published by SellerDeck Ltd.

CONTENTS

PREFACE

There's not much doubt nowadays that selling online is the fastest growing sales channel in the retail sector. Many businesses want a bigger slice of the action but it's getting more and more competitive. As a result, it's good to keep up with the latest trends but it's also important to get the basics right.

Since 1996, SellerDeck has specialised in helping small and medium sized businesses to sell on the Internet, and tens of thousands of businesses have got started with SellerDeck including many famous names. In fact, since we started we estimate that £11bn of sales have been made over the Internet using SellerDeck technology.

In this guide we share the basic steps to setting up shop on the web, together with the key lessons we have learned that can make the difference between success and failure. (For more information about SellerDeck products and services, see the SellerDeck web site).We've organised the document as a series of practical tips under different headings, so that it's easy to dip in and out of particular topics. We hope that you find this format helpful.

INTRODUCTION TO SELLING ONLINE

INTRODUCTION TO SELLING ONLINE

STEPS FOR SETTING UP AN ONLINE STORE

There's nothing that beats experience, and hopefully anyone contemplating selling online is already a web buyer. The single best bit of advice is always to put yourself in your customer's shoes – so what do you look for when you buy online?

1 FIRST, GET INFORMED.

The more you know, the better decisions you will make. So look out for articles about ecommerce in the press and online and attend a trade show or two. Most importantly, talk to people who are already selling online and think carefully about your own experiences as an online buyer.

2 CHOOSE YOUR PRODUCTS.

If you have an existing business, you are already committed to a certain area of the market and you already know or have a good idea if they will sell online. If you are selling goods that customers do not need to touch, taste or smell before buying, at a fixed price, then the web is the place to be – especially if your products are hard for customers to find. The number one reason for customers shopping online is convenience, so there is always a market for a smart operator, but the less competition the better. You can check out the competition by looking on Google for some of the products that you plan to sell.

3 GET YOUR OFFERING RIGHT.

Think about why people would want to buy from you. This might be because you have a greater range, better service or provide more comprehensive information about your products. At the end of the day, you need to provide them something which they believe will offer more value than the amount they pay, and which you can supply at a profit. It's as simple (and difficult) as that.

4 KEEP CONTROL OF THE COST.

Spending on technology is not good of itself. If you can economise on tech, you can spend more on promoting your site and bringing in customers. Avoid expensive solutions that lock you into your supplier, particularly if they are bespoke solutions that will cost a fortune every time they are updated.

5 USE TECHNOLOGY THAT ALREADY WORKS.

Use technology that works, not stuff that's a masterpiece in progress. Why bother debugging software written from scratch or extensively modified, when you could be using an application that is already working on thousands of online stores?

6 MAKE SURE EVERYTHING IS RELIABLE.

Your online store will be able to take orders 24 hours a day – but only if it is available. Depending on whether the cart is hosted you may need a third party to host your web site. Either way, make sure that your store will be very reliable. Get a personal recommendation from someone you know, or ask the supplier for their availability figures, and what they do to make sure that these stay high.

7 CONSIDER THE OWNERSHIP ISSUE.

We have heard horror stories about the treatment that some merchants have received from their ecommerce providers. If you buy a solution that is fully hosted across the net, you are dependent on your provider, and the business that you painstakingly built could be gone in a flash. This can happen if the supplier has quality or financial problems or the supplier falls out with you. Check out any problems by searching on the Internet before committing your future business to someone that might not be trustworthy. Look at the longevity and track record of the supplier before making your decision.

8 MAKE SECURITY A PRIORITY.

Both you and your customers need to feel confident that you have adequate protection against hacking and fraud. Choose an ecommerce solution that takes this seriously and has a well developed track record. The industry standard is PCI DSS (Payment Card Industry Data Encryption Standard) so make sure that your provider is fully equipped in this field. There's more advice on this later on.

9 CHOOSE AN APPROPRIATE PAYMENT SOLUTION.

In virtually every market, it's vital to be able to take card payments. Look for a range of well priced options to meet this need. There's more about this later in the book.

10 DECIDE: MARKETPLACE OR OWN WEB STORE?

The last few years have seen the rise of "online market places" such as eBay and Amazon. You can use their technology to start selling straight away and more importantly, they will deliver visitors to your store from day one. These are major benefits and are the reason why huge numbers of merchants have started selling online through this route. Many merchants with their own web sites also sell through Amazon, eBay and others. There is a whole section devoted to this topic later on.

11 DO IT YOURSELF – OR NOT?

If you decide to run your own store, then you need to decide whether you or your team can set this up yourselves or whether to use a professional. The decision whether to go it alone will depend on a variety of issues. These include your budget, your level of technical knowledge and familiarity with the Internet, the availability of technical staff within your organisation, the amount of customisation you require, the amount of time you have available and whether you enjoy playing with technology. An ecommerce package can enable you to deploy a good-looking, fully functional site quickly at low cost. A web designer will add a professional finish and, if they manage the whole project, can add enhanced features that can generate confidence and boost sales. Either way, make sure the finished site is easy to use for both you and your customers.

12 DON'T FORGET THE SALES AND MARKETING.

It is all very well opening your shop on the Internet, but you need to think about how customers are going to find you and how you will persuade them to buy. They are probably the most crucial points so we devote a major part of the book to these subjects.

INTRODUCTION TO SELLING ONLINE

THE MOST FREQUENTLY ASKED QUESTIONS ABOUT SELLING ON THE INTERNET

In this section we try to answer at a high level the basic questions that many merchants ask before they start selling online.

13 HOW CAN YOU TAKE CARD PAYMENTS ACROSS THE NET?

There are several ways that merchants can take card details securely across the net.

If you are just starting out in business, the best way to take payments is through PayPal. This is generally low cost and easy to set up. PayPal enables buyers to use their credit or debit cards as well as using any balance in their PayPal accounts.

The second option is to process card payments in real time on the Internet through your own merchant account. Once you have established your business, this is usually cheaper than using PayPal for all payments, but you do need "merchant status". This is available from all of the major banks, and they will charge a percentage of each credit card payment, and normally a fixed charge per debit transaction. You then use a "Payment Service Provider" (PSP) to link your web site, the online buyers and your merchant account. Providers offering this service include SellerDeck Payments, WorldPay, Authorize.Net and many others. As well as paying the bank, you also pay a small fee for each transaction to the PSP, typically 10p / 12c or less.

In the past, merchants captured card details and stored them at their site, then later processed them through a PDQ machine. This option is no longer viable as it is not allowed by bank rules and can result in heavy fines. Now, physical stores that already have merchant accounts should apply to their provider for "Internet merchant status".

14 HOW SHOULD PEOPLE PROMOTE THEIR ONLINE WEB STORE?

There are lots of ways that this can be done, but for any business there are two that should always be tried. The first is to promote the site to all existing customers. If existing customers don't know about the ability to buy online from you, they may go elsewhere. If they like your online store, they will probably tell their friends. So 'Order online at' and the web address should be on every piece of literature and advertising that a company produces.

The second is to register with search engines. The important ones are Google, Yahoo and Bing. It may take a little time, but it's free and can produce good results. If you plan to do this yourself, make sure you choose an ecommerce solution that will enable you to 'optimise' your pages for the search engines without needing a lot of technical knowledge. There is much more information about this later on.

15 WHAT ARE THE KEY THINGS TO TURN BROWSERS INTO BUYERS?

In short, remove the reasons why people might not buy. Make your web site oriented towards sales rather than marketing. When prospects are at the site, the marketing process is complete. So get on with selling. Make sure there's enough information, and probably images, to enable them to make the decision to purchase. Provide full terms and conditions – it looks more professional, and it protects you. Give your contact details, including a telephone number. It's the law, but it will also boost your sales. Explain your guarantee and returns policy – a rock solid guarantee goes a long way to persuading people to buy. Finally, explain your security and your privacy policy. Again, all of this is expanded later on.

16 WHAT ONE THING CAN IMPRESS BUYERS?

Make everything quick and easy. Use graphics effectively, not for the sake of it. Ensure your supplier has ultra reliable and fast servers with fast Internet connections. Make sure customers can find what they are looking for with a minimum of mouse clicks. Make the checkout process as easy as possible. Remember you're building a site for shoppers, not art lovers. The key is a professional site where visitors can easily find what they're looking for.

17 DO I NEED A BESPOKE SOLUTION, OR CAN I USE SOMETHING OFF THE SHELF?

Packaged or boxed ecommerce solutions are nowadays hugely powerful and flexible, and offer significant advantages over bespoke – lower cost, quicker site development, more features and greater long-term security. If you use a web designer, it is worth finding one that can develop a professional design based around a standard solution that other web designers could support. A completely custom-built site is only a good investment if you have special requirements that an out-of-the-box solution cannot fulfill. It will not only be more expensive initially, it is likely to be hugely expensive to make further changes in the future.

18 CAN I COMPETE WITH THE BIG BOYS?

The beauty of the Internet is that small businesses can compete effectively – nobody knows the size of your company from a web address. Ensure your site is attractive and professional looking. Make sure that you can fulfill orders very promptly - people expect delivery within a day or two. And look for a niche where you can beat the big boys at their own game, before you expand into wider fields.

19 WHAT SECURITY RISK DO ONLINE TRANSACTIONS INVOLVE?

Less than people think. In fact, the security risks run by web merchants are similar to those of mail-order companies. Just like them, it is sensible for merchants to put anti-fraud technology and policies in place. There's a whole section on this later on.

20 HOW MUCH WILL IT COST TO SET UP A SITE FOR SELLING ON THE NET?

The answer varies according to the sophistication and volume of the site. Although you can get a simple site online for around £20 per month ($30) plus fees to PayPal, you should also invest in design and marketing. Several years ago we surveyed our customers and found that all of the ones trading profitably had made a reasonable investment up front. You can get a good design and implementation done for a few thousand pounds or dollars provided you don't have any special requirements. It depends on your needs. Professional site design will increase your costs, but is still very affordable. Just make sure you leave enough in your budget for marketing your site. No visitors = no sales.

21 SHOULD MERCHANTS BE INDEPENDENT?

You should check that you have full control of the site and the means to update it easily. You should also check that the intellectual property rights of any designs are transferred to you. Also, it's always worth asking what protection you have if your supplier goes out of business.

22 IS ECOMMERCE PROFITABLE?

Absolutely yes! Selling online can be done on a small or large budget equally successfully. Successful start ups numbering in the tens of thousands in the UK and hundreds of thousands in the US prove it, along with lots of established businesses that have moved online too. As with all business initiatives, you need to do your research, get advice from trusted sources, decide what you can afford to spend to test the waters, and then jump!

TOP TIPS **23–153**

MARKETING YOUR WEBSITE

If your great idea is ever to be profitable, people have to know about it. So creating an online store is not enough on its own - just as getting a business telephone number and then expecting it to just ring is not realistic. To attract visitors to your web site you have to market it. Here are some pointers on how you can persuade prospects to visit your site. Remember that you don't merely want large numbers of visitors, it is visitors that are interested and will buy the things that you are selling.

There is a huge range of ways that ecommerce sites can be marketed. We immediately think of email and search engine marketing, but there are lots of other methods. For instance, some merchants still use traditional mail order methods like celebrity endorsement, product placement, PR, radio, TV, inserts, mail shots and print advertising. In this section we will however focus on online methods.

We will start with some of the basic principles of marketing an online store, then drill down into much more details on more advanced areas.

MARKETING YOUR WEBSITE

STARTER TIPS FOR ATTRACTING PEOPLE TO YOUR ONLINE STORE

---

23 TRY AND GET A WEB ADDRESS THAT MAKES SENSE.

It's worth spending some time thinking about your web site address (URL). Ideally it will be easy to remember, stand out from the crowd and communicate your message. It should be the same as your company name, or include it. Finding one that is suitable will probably take both time and a lot of investigation. Pretty much all obvious good URLs have been taken.

24 START WITH YOUR EXISTING MARKETING.

Put your web site address on your existing brochures, advertising, business cards and company letterhead. Wherever you promote your company name, promote your web address as well.

25 MAJOR ON SEARCH ENGINES.

Search engines are the number one source of new web site visitors, so it's worth investing some time in learning about them. That is why several tips sections within this book are devoted to the subject.

26 CONSIDER PAY PER CLICK (PPC) MARKETING.

Search engines allow advertising against results (on Google these appear at the top and right hand side of the page) and while there is enormous potential for spending large amounts of money, it can also be a way of super-charging your progress. It is well worth the effort of learning how to use this effectively. That is why there is a whole tips section is devoted to this subject too.

27 MAKE USE OF GOOGLE ANALYTICS.

Google Analytics will help you to understand how visitors are using your site, and will analyse where traffic is coming from which will help with optimising for search engines and pay-per-click marketing. More information can be found in the Google Analytics section.

28 USE FORUMS, BLOGS AND SOCIAL MEDIA.

There are lots of places where people hold discussions online such as forums, blogs and social media sites like Twitter and Facebook. Some of these sites will be talking about your specialty. For instance, if you sell yachting gear, there are plenty of discussions taking place about boating. Provided that you participate responsibly and provide genuinely helpful advice, you can get the chance to talk about your company, products and offerings. In fact, done skillfully, people will end up asking you for information about what you sell, and that can be really powerful. Just make sure you know the terms and conditions of each site and abide by them, to avoid tarnishing your reputation. There is a whole section on social media later, with tips particularly relating to Facebook and Twitter.

29 SPEND CAREFULLY.

There are lots of opportunities to advertise online, but many can be a waste of time. Before parting with your cash, you should use the same judgment that you would use when deciding whether to advertise in conventional media. Who will be looking at this medium and are they my target market? Getting your message in front of large numbers isn't the issue. They must be potential customers who are interested in your products. Unfortunately there are a lot of 'scamsters' around, so always conduct a search in Google on the company name of any supplier you are considering before making any commitment. This particularly applies if you receive an unsolicited approach.

30 ASK THE QUESTION, WHAT'S WORKING?

It's a sad fact that when it comes to marketing, the anoraks are in the driving seat. Although being creative is crucial, the way to success is to measure the results and put the next round of money where you got the most results last time. So measure everything you do, and try to find out where all your leads and customers come from. When visitors buy from your site, make sure you post a question there asking how they heard about you, or use technology that tracks this automatically. As a general rule, you should use a quarter of your capacity for testing new ideas and variations.

31 FIND SITES THAT ARE COMPLEMENTARY TO YOURS AND OFFER MUTUAL LINKS.

If you can, find specialist sites that cater for your particular niche, and get them to either link to you or put you in their search results. In return, put a link back to them. This can offer added value to your visitors as well as boosting your traffic – it's a win-win situation. It should give you more traffic through the link, and also lift your ranking in the search engines, giving more traffic that way as well. You could also set up your own referral scheme so that the linking site receives a share of the sales that they generate. The downside of this is that you need to buy some software or a service to do this.

32 USE A COMMERCIAL REFERRAL SCHEME.

There are also a number of referral schemes run commercially that you can join for a fee, and then pay a reward for clickthroughs or sales. Some sites report that this is their most cost-effective method of acquiring sales, but it will depend on what industry you are in.

33 GENERATE PR INTEREST.

Many of our customers have gained national coverage because they have an interesting story. Several have been on the TV program "Dragon's Den" and another is selling products for left handed people. If you can get the press interested, it's worth a fortune in marketing.

34 LEARN FROM THE SUCCESS OF OTHERS.

Keep an eye on your competitors, and on successful sites in other market sectors. Don't just copy them; but do learn from what they are doing, and think about how you can adapt good ideas in appropriate ways. Trawl magazines and ecommerce suppliers' web sites for case studies, and find out what other sites attribute their success to.

35 PROVIDE SOME ADDITIONAL VALUE AT YOUR SITE.

Can you come up with material for your site that will attract visitors? At SellerDeck, we provide free advice on ecommerce and the suitability of businesses for trading online, and other useful content. It's worth trying to do something similar at your site.

36 REMEMBER EXISTING CUSTOMERS.

Once you are up and running, remember that existing customers are your best customers. Make sure that you encourage them to return by making special offers and letting them know what you are doing at your store.

37 USE EMAIL MARKETING.

There are now many responsible companies offering information and services relating to email marketing. They can supply email lists, advice and delivery technology. They will ensure that you comply with the law, for instance by only sending marketing emails to individuals that have opted in to receive them. With email marketing it is often useful to reward a response - for example by offering a discount for people that click through. There is a whole section on email marketing as it has so much potential to grow sales.

38 SHOW YOUR APPRECIATION FOR RECOMMENDATIONS.

Ask your customers to recommend you to their friends. You are much more likely to make a sale if recommended by someone trusted. If you get a sale as a result of a recommendation and the volumes make it possible, say thank you personally and send some form of reward – whether it is a small gift or a voucher that can be used at your store.

39 GET CUSTOMER FEEDBACK.

Increasingly, prospects expect to see what other people thought of your products and service, so gather this information on your site. If this can be gathered by an independent third party, so much the better. Customers are rightly cynical and will be much more influenced if they believe you haven't been able to fiddle with the results. There's more about this later.

40 RECOVER THE ONES THAT GOT AWAY.

As well as acquiring new customers, you should have a strategy for recovering potential customers that were lost. Your ecommerce solution should provide you with the details of customers that filled in their details but failed to complete the order by making a payment.

41 MARKET OFFLINE.

It's true that all of your prospects are online (if they are not online, they can't buy from your store!) But it's sometimes forgotten that 100% of these prospects also have a life offline. You need to ask whether traditional marketing methods such as direct mail may drive traffic cost-effectively to your site.

MARKETING YOUR WEBSITE

ANALYTICS – UNDERSTAND THE TRAFFIC ON YOUR SITE

Marketing on the Internet is very different from many other types of marketing, in that everything can be measured. The problem that many people make is that they fail to measure. That's why we have put implementing Google Analytics ahead of both search engine marketing and pay-per-click marketing. You need to be able to have the ability to measure the results of your activities before you actually carry them out. In this section we explain a number of aspects of that wonderful free tool – Google Analytics.

42 APPRECIATE THE VALUE OF ANALYTICS.

There are many Analytics providers offering a variety of services at a variety of prices. The most popular is Google Analytics, which is a free service supplied by Google. Understanding the importance of using Analytics will in time help you to build and grow your website and allow you to generate greater financial returns.

43 REGISTER AS AN ECOMMERCE SITE.

Google Analytics has an 'Ecommerce' option. Activating this will allow Google Analytics to not only follow your traffic, but your sales and conversions as well. The Google Analytics Ecommerce option puts a monetary value on conversions allowing you to quickly see the real value of your site.

44 TARGET AND ADAPT.

Using Google Analytics, have a look at the inbound links and subsequent sources bringing traffic to your site. If there are any new links, or particular high traffic from a particular link, you can see which page they are landing on. By then viewing the host page of that link, you can see what that audience is hoping to find by visiting your site. You can then optimise that page to make sure that it's laid out for what they will want to find.

45 OPTIMISE FOR THE MOST POPULAR BROWSERS.

Not everyone uses the same browser. Generally, people will be using one of the most popular three or four browsers, all of which have several versions. Older or newer versions may display different websites in a way other than intended. Use Google Analytics to see which versions of which browsers your prospects are using. You can also check to see if any browsers have a higher bounce rate i.e. they leave your site as soon as they arrive. This would indicate that there were some issues with that particular browser.

46 SET GOALS AND TARGETS.

A goal is completed when one of your customers completes a desired action whilst on your website, such as making a purchase, downloading a file, signing up for a mailing list or viewing a certain page. You can set up as many goals as you wish and track the progress of these over time. This is especially handy for marketing and advertising campaigns. Goals are particularly useful too for measuring non-transactional activity.

47 INTEGRATE WITH SOCIAL MEDIA.

Understand the importance of not just listening to and communicating with your customers via social networks, but following the performance of your social networks using Google Analytics. When you post or Tweet offers, discounts or links, find out which ones have performed better than others to maximise on the potential for future traffic. Use the 'Social' tab for a full break down of how social networks are working for you. There are whole sections on using social media elsewhere.

48 WORK ON YOUR KEYWORDS.

You should already know the value of optimising your site for search engines and making sure you optimise for certain search keywords is a vital part of this. There are whole sections on this elsewhere. You can use Google Analytics to track the results of how much traffic your site is receiving from these keywords. Doing further work on the keywords that bring the most traffic already is likely to have the largest impact.

49 USE CUSTOM REPORTS.

Although Google Analytics has many 'ready made' reports and lays out the data in an easy to understand way, Custom Reporting is also a great tool. You can choose from a variety of Metrics and Dimensions to create reports that give you exactly what you want to know. For example, you could set up a report telling you your bounce rates, compared to browser type or even location.

50 MAKE SURE YOUR SITE IS FAST.

Google Analytics displays which pages are taking longer to load than others. Research has shown that 40% of online shoppers abandon completely if they have to wait for more than 3 seconds for a page to load. Identify the 'slow loaders' and make sure that they are fixed.

51 CONCENTRATE ON TRENDS.

Once problem areas have been identified and changes made, continue to compare your analytics week on week or month on month. If you see positive or negative trends in your traffic you can act accordingly. It is easy to get bogged down by looking at your visitors and other statistics on a day-to-day basis but it is best to track trends over time. If you are not seeing increases then you know there may be problems to look into.

52 STAY LIVE.

Google Analytics now offers 'Real-Time', a live overview of who is on your site, right now. Throughout your day, keep this open and you will be able to react immediately to any differing activity in traffic without having to wait until the next day, when it could be too late.

53 UNDERSTAND WHY PEOPLE ARE LEAVING.

Create a Custom Report with the Metric 'Exits' and the Dimension as 'Page'. The results for this will show you exactly which pages on your site the most people leave from. Hopefully, this will be your order confirmation page. If however, a certain page has an unusually high exit rate, view the page and find out why. You can then fix any problems and compare the same data in the future.

54 DON'T LET YOUR LANDERS BOUNCE.

Under the Site Content tab, have a look at your landing page, which is the initial page your site visitor lands on. Keep an eye on the bounce rate, as a high bounce rate indicates people aren't going on to browse through your site, but ending their interest there. If browsers get no further than your first page you are wasting your marketing efforts. So experiment to try to minimise the bounce rate.

55 WATCH BOTH NEW AND RETURN VISITS.

Keeping your content regularly updated will encourage return visits. This can be done with new products, updated product information or reviews as well as blog posts and competitions for example. Ideally, your site should have a healthy balance of new and returning visitors. This will provide good growth with new visits adding to repeat visits.

56 USE GOOGLE'S FREE LEARNING TOOLS.

Google has lots of free documents and videos on how to get the most out of Google Analytics. Spend some time educating yourself and becoming an expert; the tips and tricks you learn will become invaluable to your business.

57 TAKE ANALYTICS WITH A PINCH OF SALT.

Although the information and data available is incredible, with a vast array of knowledge, it is not perfect. Analytics uses cookies stored on the end users computer. Cookies can be deleted and cleared, so Analytics would see that visitor as a 'new' visit, rather than a 'returning visit'. Also, Analytics will include your own visits and activity on your website. For instance, if you have your own website open in your browser all day, the 'average time on site' will be very high.

MARKETING YOUR WEBSITE

SEARCH ENGINE MARKETING – GETTING THE BASICS RIGHT

It may sound obvious, but search engines are the number one source of new visitors to websites. According to comScore, over ninety percent of UK Internet users use them, and over eighty percent of those use Google.

Also, eighty percent of users do not look beyond the first page of search engine results. That means if your site is not on the first page, you will hardly be noticed. So make sure that you have a plan, drawn from the next three sections, to get at least some relevant presence on the first page.

There are two ways of getting people to visit your site from search engines. 'Natural' or 'organic' listings are the results which the search engine itself has determined are most relevant. 'Pay per click' or 'sponsored' listings are advertisements which appear at the top and on the right of the search engine results when certain specified words have been searched for. The merchant pays each time a searcher clicks on an advert. The good news is that everyone who comes to your site by either method is probably searching for the products that you sell.

When we search on Google or other search engines, we are searching for something specific. We may type a single word or several keywords. We may search once, then try again with a different search. The job of every merchant is to find out what their potential customers are searching for. It's not just about numbers, it's about relevance as there is no point in getting people to visit your site if they will never buy. You need to attract real prospects.

The most popular search engines and search advertising networks worldwide are Google, Yahoo, Bing (from Microsoft), Ask and Miva (US only). The tips here are oriented towards Google, but are also useful with the other search engines.

The tips are split into three sections: identifying keywords and deciding whether to target them in the natural (SEO) or paid listings (PPC), then a section on each of these two approaches. This is a subject that is very much seen as a black art, but as you will see, many of the principles are fairly straight-forward.

IDENTIFY YOUR KEY WORDS AND BALANCE SEO AND PPC

In this section we will focus on working on what's being searched for and what to target, with separate sections for implementing your search engine optimisation (SEO) and paid marketing (pay per click or PPC) strategies.

58 UNDERSTAND THE KEYWORD PROCESS.

Keywords (which can also be phrases) are critical to succeeding with search engine marketing because they are what people are actually searching for - it's what they type into the search box. Successful use of keywords involves expanding on an initial list, understanding the volume of traffic for each keyword, understanding how competitive these are and coming up with a plan to target a selection. Each topic is expanded in the tips below.

59 BRAINSTORM AN INITIAL LIST.

Make sure you take enough time to select keywords. It's good to get some initial ideas from brainstorming the terms that you would search on if you were looking for the products that you sell. Also look at competitor's sites and note the words they use in the page titles that appear at the top of your browser when you view their site.

60 EXPAND YOUR LIST.

Once you have a list you need to expand it as there will be lots of variants and related ways of searching that you hadn't thought of. Avoid single words like 'shoes' or very broad terms like 'groceries'. There will be so many sites in these kinds of category that you will be very unlikely to get ranked on the first or even second pages.

61 USE ONLINE RESOURCES TO FURTHER EXPAND AND DETERMINE VOLUMES.

You also need to determine the volume of searches on each term. The following resources can help:
https://adwords.google.com/select/KeywordToolExternal Free. Once you have a Google Adwords account you can access additional resources.
http://www.keyworddiscovery.com Free trial, paid normal use.
http://www.hitwise.co.uk Paid, but has some free statistics. It bases its analysis on major UK ISPs, so is biased more towards analysing consumer rather business buyers.
http://www.wordtracker.com Free trial, paid normal use.

62 UNDERSTAND THE COMPETITION.

By entering keywords into Google, you can determine two things. The first is how many search results there are in total for the particular words, which Google reports back along with the first page of results. Secondly you can see on the results page how many adverts there are. In general, the more adverts there are (particularly at the top of the page), and the more search results, the more competitive the keywords. You are looking for keywords that have a lower ratio of competitive results to traffic, as these represent the best opportunities.

63 TRY A PAY-PER-CLICK (PPC) ADVERTISING TEST WITH GOOGLE OR YAHOO.

PPC ads can be useful and cost-effective traffic generators in their own right, but here we are talking about a small scale (and limited cost) test to both gain familiarisation and to test the water. PPC works a bit like an auction. You put a bid in on the amount you are prepared to pay, and Google will place your ad mostly by comparing your bid with the competition, with higher bids appearing higher up the page. You only pay when a searcher actually clicks on your advert. Getting an idea of the workings of this is crucial. PPC attracts fewer clicks than natural or 'organic' listings and is generally much more expensive than optimising your site. However, you can get a "double whammy" by using PPC to both test whether PPC is cost-effective for you and also testing out how much traffic and sales you get from various key words. In fact with a new site it is probably worth using a PPC ad for a few weeks, limiting it to one or two pounds a day, as this seems to get Google to visit your site more frequently which should improve your ranking.

64 DECIDE ON WHAT WILL BE TARGETED IN SEO AND WHAT IN PPC.

You might choose to target high cost keywords in SEO rather than PPC, or if profitable, you might do this the other way around or using both. This will depend on which approach will yield profitable results. Every company will be different. For instance, depending on the lifetime value of a customer, a higher cost PPC campaign may work for one company but not for another. Large companies may get kick-backs for advertising through their agency, lowering their relative costs. Research by the Atlas Institute (Microsoft) has shown that prospects exposed to both search results and display ads from the same company are more likely to purchase. There are whole sections on PPC and SEO below.

65 WORK TO YOUR TIMELINE.

Pay per click advertising can start producing results immediately, but search engine optimisation can take months before any impact is made, especially as you can be stuck in Google's "sandbox" for some time while Google appears to be thinking whether to list you or not. Search engines are businesses too, and the quickest way to get listed is to pay them. Consider this if your timelines require it.

66 MANAGE KEYWORDS AS A CRITICAL ASSET.

Keep a master list of your keywords (and phrases) and track results against them. Redo your keyword analysis regularly e.g. every three or six months, to ensure that you change your marketing in line with customer trends. Remember seasonal variations e.g. Christmas, Spring, Valentine's Day, the World Cup, end of accounting year, new competition, new products etc. Rank top keywords by the results you get.

67 MATCH YOUR PROPOSITION.

You may choose not to target "Cheap", "Discount" or "Clearance" due to the mindset of the person searching, and how it matches your business proposition. If it does match, you may specifically target these words in tandem with other keywords. The point is that you should achieve better conversion when the searcher is aligned with the way that you do business.

68 BE UNIQUE.

To distinguish yourself, one approach is to try to offer something that really sets you apart. It may be a unique range of products, special arrangements, some expert advice, or even a combination of products. You can then optimise your site on keywords around this specialisation, which can be much more cost effective. The message here is that the more you specialise, the less the competition. If you can identify a new trend and be the only business selling a product for a while, this can also be very profitable. This doesn't need to be complicated, one of SellerDeck's customers spotted a major retailer selling a new product very successfully, but not stocking the spares. They sourced the spares and got them online, then bam – there was an immediate stream of orders.

69 TARGET ALL RELEVANT TRAFFIC.

Remember that you want to make sure that people searching specifically for you find you. So as well as looking at the products you sell and your proposition, target your own brand and probably competitor brands too e.g. Renault cars, Audi cars.

70 CONSIDER THE LONG TAIL.

In recent years, a new expression – "the long tail" has emerged in business circles. In the context of PPC advertising, this is about advertising on lots of keywords that are rarely searched for, but can collectively add up to a lot of traffic. Companies have been known to use over 5,000 different groups of keywords because hard work pays off. Rarer keywords tend to be cheaper and convert better.

71 USE VARIANTS.

Use words in both the singular and plural as well as putting words in different orders as these are all regarded as different searches. Find synonyms. You may do this yourself, or let Google do it for you using its broader matching. Remember you may put brands into the keywords. Highly refined keywords tend to indicate a real intention to purchase, as do words like "Buy". Don't just choose the obvious.

MARKETING YOUR WEBSITE

SEARCH ENGINE OPTIMISATION (SEO)

The natural or organic listings in the main body of the search results are both popular with searchers and free for your company. The bad news is that you have no direct control over when you will appear or where you will come in the pecking order. To try to get to the top, optimise on a limited set of keywords, selected as described in the previous section. In competitive markets, it's better to do well on a keyword that only a moderate number of people search on, than to do badly on a keyword that is more popular.

Remember that the search engines have spent billions tuning their algorithms to try and find the most relevant sites for each keyword. So the general advice is to try to make your site relevant – that way you are working with them rather than against them. This means having a planet of genuine and useful content related to your keywords. Here you use rich media such as images and videos which are likely to score well in the long run.

72 MANUALLY SUBMIT YOUR PAGES TO YOUR TARGET SEARCH ENGINES,

making sure you include the major search providers listed below. Don't worry about the hundreds of others, and don't believe any pitch that emphasises them. Having said that, there might be a small number of specialist directories that are particularly relevant to your category.

The key search engines in priority order are:

- Google
- Yahoo! (websites and directory)
- Bing (Microsoft)
- Ask
- Open Directory (dmoz.org)

73 MAKE THE MOST OF YOUR DOMAIN.

Google trusts domains more as the length of time that they have been registered increases. So it may be worth doing some research and seeing if you can purchase an existing domain that is relevant to your market segment. If you can't, get some pages loaded up on your domain ahead of launch and then register them with Google. This way you will get a faster start when you are finally ready to go. Google also takes into account whether any keywords occur as part of your domain name when ranking your site. So take that into account.

74 BIG IS BETTER.

Google prefers a large site with many pages to a small site with few pages. Try to get plenty of content on your site but make sure that it is useful and duplication is minimised.

75 MAKE SURE YOUR SITE CONTENT CHANGES FREQUENTLY.

Google considers that sites where the content changes all the time are of a higher quality. So make sure that you put the effort into making that true for you.

76 HAVE A FAST SITE.

Google ranks fast sites higher. Amazon reckons that every 100 milliseconds delay to your site reduces customer activity by 1%. So speed matters. There are three parts to making your site fast: the quality of your hosting, the architecture of your ecommerce shopping cart and the total size of all of the content on each web page. You can usually considerably reduce the size of your content by making sure that you don't overdo the number and size of images and experimenting with using images of different types - jpegs, gifs or png files. You should also consider use of gzip compression on your site. Your site provider should be able to provide details.

77 BUILD INBOUND LINKS.

One of the most important things from Google's point of view is the number and quality of links to your site, particularly if the link contains your keywords. It regards these as votes of confidence in you. As a result, some kind of program to develop reciprocal links with other sites will be essential if your optimisation strategy is to succeed. Another good way to build up a network of links is to position yourself as a special resource in your field. Maybe you can supply poems to go with your flowers, or information on the derivation of names? This type of material can act as "link bait" – something that naturally attracts links from other sites. Another way to build inbound links is by writing blogs and articles with links back to your site. Make sure that you are listed in any directories that are relevant to your industry. Many of these can be free.

78 DISTRIBUTE PRESS RELEASES ONLINE.

If you have any news to announce that could be of interest, write a press release and distribute it to the online sites that take them. Any that run your release will provide a link back to your site, and that will boost your search engine rankings.

79 INCLUDE SOCIAL NETWORKING IN YOUR STRATEGY.

There's a whole section on social networking but it is worth noting that Google is increasingly including real time feeds from social networks to try and keep results as up to date as possible.

80 USE ONLINE RESOURCES.

Google's Webmaster Tools at http://www.google.com/webmasters/ is a great first step. Paid for and free tools that you can use to check your position in search engines include http://www.webceo.com/, http://www.marketsamurai.com/, a plug in for the Firefox web browser called http://tools.seobook.com/firefox/rank-checker/ and free tool http://speedyseo.com/seo-tool.

81 DON'T PUT TOO MANY KEYWORDS ON ONE PAGE.

It's impossible to make every page rank for every keyword. The way to solve this is to optimise different pages for different sets of keywords.

82 INCLUDE THE KEYWORDS EARLY IN THE TITLE TAG.

Different search engines take different things into account when deciding their priorities. Google attaches particular importance to page title – the text that appears in the top of the browser when you view the page. In the HTML code, it is the text between the <TITLE> and </TITLE> tags. The title should be no longer than nine words. For example, suppose you are running a sailing site and you have decided that 'boats for sale' and 'yachts for sale' are the keywords your potential customers are most likely to use. You would set up your meta tags something like this:

<HEAD>
<TITLE>Boats for sale and yachts for sale from Seven Seas Sailing</TITLE> - This title is longer than 9 words – suggest "Boats and Yachts for sale from Seven Seas Sailing"
<META Name='description' Content='boats for sale, yachts for sale and everything you need to know about sailing'>
<META Name='keywords' Content='boats for sale yachts for sale sailing sails">
</HEAD>

Good ecommerce packages will do this for you with no need to edit the HTML, although there should be an option to do so.

83 REPEAT THE KEYWORDS.

Google analyses how many times the keywords appear on the page; where it appears (near the top is better than near the bottom); and whether occurrences of the keywords are spread out over the page, or concentrated in one place. Work your keywords naturally several times throughout the text of the page, starting from the top. If your page is based on a table, this will mean placing them near the top of the left-hand column.

84 WORK THE KEYWORDS INTO EVERYTHING.

Keywords should appear in heading tags – the h1 tag – and in the URL, the image names, image Alt tags, internal link names and file names. Add a Meta Description tag (as shown in an earlier tip), but don't worry about Meta Keyword tags unless you know you will be targeting a search engine that uses them. Most don't. Good ecommerce packages will optimise your site automatically with no need to edit HTML.

85 ACT NATURAL.

Don't try to conceal keywords, for example by putting them in small or white text or in the same colour as the background and don't 'spam' by repeating keywords mindlessly; you may be blacklisted irrevocably by the search engines for using this kind of trick. In fact, any one set of keywords should never exceed 5% of the total text. Avoid automated submission tools and "Link farms". Often taking part in this activity can result in your site getting demoted in the search engines.

86 CONSIDER CONCENTRATING ON SMALLER SEARCH ENGINES.

If you operate in a market where there is a lot of traffic through search engines and a lot of competition, consider concentrating your effort on smaller search engines. You may get better results for the same expenditure, and the overall market volume means that there are still good pickings, even from the smallest engines.

87 SEE HOW YOU ARE DOING.

However smart you are with your marketing, you can always improve. To monitor performance, use a free tool like Google Analytics. Studying what works is vital to getting the best from these activities. Understanding how search engines work in your space is not trivial, but isn't beyond most of us. Time spent on learning and action will pay off directly in sales.

88 USE SPECIALISTS BUT DON'T BE CONNED.

There are many specialists that offer search engine optimisation (SEO) who can help to improve your rankings, but there are also many cowboys with big charges and poor delivery. Avoid the scam where a supplier offers you "guaranteed top rankings" or the certainty of being on page one of Google. No-one can guarantee top rankings except for keywords that aren't important and will generate hardly any traffic, so that's what you will get. The advice in this section and the previous one should help you make a good start if you optimise your site for yourself. Alternatively, if you use a third party, it will help you keep tabs on them and make sure they are advising you well.

MARKETING YOUR WEBSITE

MAXIMISE PAY-PER-CLICK CAMPAIGNS

In this section we look much more closely at paid advertising through search engines. This is where your ads are displayed either at the top or down the right hand side based on the keywords that the prospect is searching for. This is a huge multi-billion business in both the US and UK. There are a number of different engines, but again the dominant one is Google. Most search engines allow both advertising on the engine itself, and also on a network of associated sites. You can choose whether to include or exclude these from your advertising.

Unlike search engine optimisation (SEO), paid marketing produces faster results and is more under your control. We've seen thousands of web businesses start up and many become highly successful. A good chunk of these achieved their outstanding results through pay-per-click (PPC) campaigns used both aggressively and effectively. However, it costs money and producing the best results takes a lot of effort.

The way that search advertising generally works is that you select keywords along with a maximum amount you are prepared to pay for someone to click through to your site. When those keywords are entered in the search box by the person searching, the search engine decides which ads to display in which order based on the bids and some other rules. You get charged if a searcher clicks on your ad – hence the term "pay per click".

The tips here will concentrate on Google, however, practically all of them also apply to the other search engines with slight differences.

89 LEARN BEFORE YOU SPEND.

Nobody would fancy their chances in a martial arts contest if they had never fought before, or in a high stakes poker game if they had never played. With search engine advertising it's similar. At least learn the basics before you spend more than experimental pin money. It's easy to waste a lot of money and damage your ratings in Google's eyes if you don't know what you are doing. Help is available at the adwords blog http://adwords.blogspot.com/ and http://adwords.google.com/support/ where you can search on Adwords help. You can also get involved in forums where PPC is discussed. Although we can provide many pointers here, the field is always evolving and every so often new insights emerge.

90 CONSIDER THE STRUCTURE OF AD GROUPS, ADS, PAGES, AND KEYWORDS.

Google allows you to create campaigns, groups of adverts, define your keywords and create individual advertisements (Ads). A campaign consists of one or more ad groups and an ad group consists of one or more keywords and one or more ads. Each ad points to a single page on your site. Bids (bid, max amount per month etc) can be set at campaign or ad group level. Matching rules, which are explained below, can be set for each set of keywords. It's best to base each Ad Group around a common theme but have less than 15-20 keywords per ad group. Developing many more focused Ad Groups will give better results but is more work. Don't use the same keywords in different Ad Groups as they compete against each other and it makes the results difficult to understand. Think about whether you wish to advertise on words like compare, low cost, cheap, discount, discounted or whether you wish to exclude searches including them. All of this will all become much clearer as you try some actual PPC campaigns.

91 UNDERSTAND THE AD RULES.

Creating good Ads is hard. You have just 25 characters for the headline, 35 each for the two description lines and 25 for the display URL. Microsoft are the same, Yahoo and Miva have longer ads. You are not allowed exclamation marks in the headline and not too much capitalisation or punctuation. Style guides can be found on the relevant ad network's site.

92 MAKE ADS EFFECTIVE.

Your Ads appear with the competition, so they have to stand out. But you don't just want clicks, you want clicks from people who will buy. You should take time in crafting and experimenting with Ads. Ask who is the ad targeted at? Who are the competition? How can you motivate people to click? What tone do you wish to adopt? What are your benefits? Should you include your brand in the headline? What provocative question can you ask? How can you establish credibility? Try to look like you provide better value or a broader offering than the competition.

93 TRY OUT DIFFERENT IDEAS.

Here are some ideas to help: include the search terms in your ad copy by using dynamic keyword insertion as follows {KeyWord:<Default Phrase>}; emphasise what you can offer for "Free", e.g. free shipping, free insurance, free guide. Demonstrate your credibility and points of difference as a supplier, achieve impact through visual tricks like first-letter capitalisation, ampersands and use of quotation marks; consider including price or price range. Try using verbs implying action like Find, Win, Act Now, Buy, Get, See, Save. State the benefits followed by a call to action.

94 VARY THE DISPLAY URL.

The URL displayed at the end of the Ad must broadly indicate where the click will go but does not have to reflect the exact URL that will be followed when the ad is clicked. So use this capability. In the display URL consider capitalising the brand name, remove www, add a product name or a call to action on the end or put in the country e.g. SellerDeck.co.uk/SellerDeckExpress or SellerDeck.co.uk/Special-Deals.html. There are documented cases of doubling the click through rate simply by changing this URL description.

95 UNDERSTAND THE GOOGLE QUALITY SCORE AND MAXIMISE IT.

Google and other search engines calculate a "quality score" for your adverts and this (along with the amount that you bid) determines the order in which adverts appear. In other words, a good quality score can enable you to achieve the same results with less money. Google does not divulge its precise calculation, but does take the following factors into account to calculate the score: the extent to which the search terms match your advert; the same with the URL and the content of the landing page the searcher will click through to; the percentage of people who click on your advert after seeing it (the click through rate or CTR). The CTR is the most important of these and Google takes into account the ad position as higher positions naturally get higher CTRs.

96 BUILD GOOD LANDING PAGES.

It's worth creating specific landing pages for different ads both to maximise sales and because the relevance of the landing page impacts the quality score. Google re-evaluates landing pages once per month. For landing page to be relevant (so impacting the quality score) they should be fast, have a relevant title, and have keywords in the text (but these should be less than 5%). If there are text hyperlinks containing keywords that helps too. However, if visitors arriving at your page immediately follow this by another Google search, you will be marked down as you obviously weren't relevant. Remember to communicate positively and ideally have a call to action on the page e.g. "buy" or have a prominent phone number if your objective is to get them to call. You can choose whether to have landing pages specifically for incoming traffic from PPC or use your existing standard pages. Either way, you must not use doorway pages with no links from the rest of the site. If you had a theme of advertising based on value, then you might have a landing page emphasising how you deliver this proposition e.g. free shipping. You can find your quality score from within your Google Adwords account.

97 UNDERSTAND THE MATCHING RULES.

Each search engine has its own rules on which ads will be triggered by searches on which keywords. You control matches by specifying your own keywords and how these should be matched to what's being searched. On Google, a "phrase match" uses quotes (" ") around your keywords and an "exact match" uses square brackets ([ ]), otherwise it's a "broad match". You need to understand how the matching rules work. For instance, beware on insisting on an exact match as you may exclude plurals but also beware of broad matches which may unexpectedly lead to higher spend and irrelevant traffic. You should also use negative matching which is where keywords will not match if a particular negative word is also being searched for. Using negatives can increase click through rates and reduce costs from irrelevant clicks and can be applied at campaign level.

When quotes are used which signifies phrase matching (Google and Bing) then this will match with searchers who use the particular keywords along with additional words before or after. An exact match [square brackets] matches only when those exact keywords in the exact order with no additional words are searched for. Because it's difficult, you may be able to out-perform the competition by detailed understanding and hard work.

98 PLAN YOUR MATCHING CAREFULLY.

In general, you should define keywords with three or more words as a broad match and keywords with one or two words as a phrase match. Beware that the lower click through rate (CTR) arising from broad matches will lower your quality score. There is a trade-off between impression volume and the relevance of your ad since your creative may be less relevant for keywords which are not so closely associated. For example a recruitment agency might advertise for "Ruby Programming Jobs" with a broad match. The ad will be displayed when the searcher searches on other types of jobs such as "Java Programming Jobs" and "PHP Programming Jobs" and this may not be at all what the advertiser expected. As a result, a minimum of three word keywords should be used for a broad match. Try to report on keywords searched upon that never got a click and get rid of non-performing ads. If you combine match types then the search engine selects the most relevant one in the order of exact, phrase and broad match. Remember to put in a negative for things in your field that you don't sell.

99 TARGET YOUR POSITION.

In general, the higher position that your ad appears on the search results page, the more clicks you will get. The biggest determiner of the position you appear is the amount you bid. The less important factor is the quality score and other tips explain how to improve this. There is an optimum amount to bid that will balance the cost you pay per click with the amount of traffic you receive. One twist is that not all lower positions are equal. If there are three "sponsored results" above the organic listings, then the fourth position will be at the top right, which is likely to be advantageous. You can set a position preference in Google – this may well be worth doing, particularly to get position 4 in the situation described above. Specifying position can sharply reduce how often your ad is shown, as bids will be lowered but not raised to achieve the target. Having said that you could bid very high along with setting the position. Remember that conversion rates can be higher for lower positions if you have a more relevant ad than the higher ranked competition. Traffic drops by around 10% for each lower position and by more at the top – typically 30% from first to second and 20% from second to third.

100 SET YOUR BUDGET AND BIDDING RULES.

Once everything above has been understood, you are able to produce a plan, which should consist of your budget, how you will bid, and maximum amounts for the day and week or month. Look at what competitors are doing, you may be able to run your PPC campaign at the end of the day, week or month when competitor's budgets have expired and you can bid much lower for a good position.

101 REGULARLY ASSESS PROFITABILITY.

Work out the profitability of PPC advertising, as it's equally easy to spend too much, too little or suffer from competitors who are behaving very smartly or very stupidly.

102 UNDERSTAND HOW ADS ARE ROTATED.

You can have more than one Ad linked together and they will be rotated evenly at first but slowly the one with higher CTR will be displayed more frequently. Look at the percentage served in the "Ad variations" table to see which is best. This is a simple form of testing Ads against each other and it suggests that new Ads should be continuously tried and less successful ones dropped. Remember that if you change an Ad you will lose your quality score so adding new Ads is probably a better way of testing. Bidding on your own brand will improve CTR performance.

103 UNDERSTAND THE NUMBERS.

Hitwise provides "Share of search", "Gap analysis" etc. Instructions on using the Report Centre to show Impression Share are here: https://adwords.google.com/support/bin/answer.py?answer=52760. Where possible, measure results dividing the cost of a click by the average sales achieved providing a cost per pound or dollar of sales. Google Analytics, integrated with your ecommerce package, should be able to help here. If this isn't possible, then cost per acquisition (CPA) i.e. cost to make each sale, or worse cost per click (CPC) can be used. Try to get the best figures by including an estimate of telephone sales influenced by the web site and if possible also take into account lifetime customer value and customer returns. All of this helps you to understand which of your activities are profitable.

104 HAVE A STRUCTURED APPROACH TO ADJUST AND TEST THINGS IN THE LIGHT OF THE NUMBERS.

The overall performance of your PPC campaign will be determined by the number of times your ads are displayed for which keywords and against which competition. Also making an impact is the position on the page the ad appears; the percentage of times that customers click on your ad and your success at converting those clicks to sales. The key to improvement is to try alternatives around each factor, testing one variable at a time. You should assess the variation in conversion rates for different keywords and seek to understand the reason for this variation – is it due to the level of intent of the keywords, the design of the landing page or the product price and details? You should then focus your search engine marketing on keywords that attract visitors that actually convert to sales. Review high volume keywords more frequently

Let the competition make themselves poor, and Google rich. Consider not bidding on the most competitive keywords, as this may well increase your profitability, but beware if this gives competitors economies of scale that you then can't achieve. Pay per click advertising can acquire customers, but as your name will be put in front of many browsers who don't click through, it could also improve your branding. If this is important, take it into account when assessing the cost versus benefit. You might prioritise some more of SEO if PPC is too competitive and expensive.

Prioritise keywords for SEO. If we are already high, then you can bid lower. Using the information that has been covered up until this point, you need to be highly pro-active in running your campaign. Delete keywords with poor or zero clickthrough to avoid dragging down overall CTRs.

105 WATCH OUT FOR CLICK FRAUD.

Around 10% of clicks can be fraudulent. These are clicks on your ads with no intention to buy. Also running searches with competitor's ads and NOT clicking on them, while perpetrators' ads are disabled, thus reducing your quality score due to lower CTR. Get complaints in within 60 days. You can get a report from Google on what they have filtered as invalid. You can choose to exclude chosen IP addresses so you can stop competitors clicking on your ads. You can set up benchmark data and if this starts getting exceeded, then present this to the search engines for investigation. Google says that they investigate all cases of fraud.

106 SPEND AGGRESSIVELY WHEN IT'S WORKING.

Once you can see that your pay per click strategy is working, then make hay while the sun shines. If you have found a winning formula, others will be along shortly to learn from your success. So grow rapidly while you can and make sure that you get the most advantage.

107 RESPOND TO COMPETITION.

Because of the nature of PPC advertising, where cost is largely dependent on competitor activity, it's important to monitor the competition. Relative to them, you may have less advantageous terms if you are smaller due to the relative cost of management of campaigns, lower lifetime values and lack of agency kick-backs. One approach is to look at both PPC and SEO campaigns together to maximise the results that you wish to get. For instance, you might focus your SEO efforts solely on high traffic key words where the cost of PPC bidding is very high, then, focus PPC efforts on less popular terms where there is a better return on investment.

108 PROTECT YOUR OWN BRAND.

If people search on your brand, you need to protect it by advertising yourself on it or by other means. You might also choose to advertise on competitor's brands. Keep up to date to ensure you are using the latest methods to protect your brand.

109 CONSIDER CONTENT NETWORKS.

In addition to advertising on search pages, you can advertise on the "Content network" so that ads show up on third party sites affiliated with the search provider. As an example, see "Ads by Google scattered around the site: www.davechaffey.com. It's well worth distinguishing between content and search advertising as they have different characteristics. Note that Google will display your ads on their content network unless you explicitly opt out. You should generally bid lower and display different ads for Content networks, probably being more provocative as people aren't explicitly searching when your ads are displayed. You should possibly promote your brand. e.g. "SellerDeck for ecommerce" as if they don't get clicked, you may still get some benefits. Always use site exclusions to avoid wasted ads. For content networks, ads are normally displayed next to content relevant to your keywords. Google is the dominant player and people rightly consider advertising on Google first. However, sometimes you can get great results by focusing on a smaller part of the market, accessed through one of Google's competitors such as Yahoo or Bing (Microsoft). The advertising network Miva displays ads on The Sun and Dennis publishing websites, which are pretty significant for some sectors.

110 CONSIDER ALL THE SEARCH ENGINES.

Details of all of the programs are at Google (http://adwords.google.com), Yahoo! (http://searchmarketing.yahoo.com) and Microsoft (http://adcenter.microsoft.com) and for Ask (www.ask.com). Help can be found at http://searchmarketing.yahoo.com/rc/srch/mt_hiw.php

MARKETING YOUR WEBSITE

USE EMAIL MARKETING

To some people, email marketing is all bad, brought about by the irritating and irresponsible activities of "spammers". However, dismissing email marketing can be a big mistake as it remains an enormously powerful medium. It's just important that the law is obeyed and that common sense prevails. This section is designed to achieve great business results while working within those constraints.

Email marketing can be used in three main ways. The first is "cold contact" where an email list is bought and an attempt made to rustle up new business. The second is where prospects have provided their email address to you, typically to receive a newsletter. The final opportunity is where the prospects have previously bought from you – so you already have some form of relationship. Although there are common principles across each of these cases, each requires separate consideration. For instance, identifying your company as the sender makes sense when they have bought before, but may be a disadvantage if they haven't.

Across all email types, there are three challenges. The first is to get your emails delivered, the second is to get them opened and the third is to achieve a business result. Each needs to be considered in turn.

111 OBEY THE RULES.

Don't communicate with people who haven't given permission. Always provide a free opt out in all your communication. Continuing to contact someone who has already opted out will infuriate people and in the modern era of social networking, can lead to a lot of negative publicity. You and your sub-contractors e.g. shipping companies are allowed to communicate with customers in order to fulfill your contract to deliver and you do not need permission for that.

112 PLAN.

Email addresses are a valuable asset, whether bought in, acquired for a newsletter, or obtained from people who have bought from your store. As a result, you should carefully plan how you will use them, as it is incredibly easy to destroy their potential. It's important that you plan any campaign properly, and not have a series of poorly thought through and ill timed communications. At all times you must keep recipients engaged with your content.

113 BUILD AN EMAIL LIST.

Provide a prominent and simple sign-up to a mailing list on every page – but only if you will actually make use of the information. Email addresses enable newsletters to be sent, which can then be used to move on by capturing more details. Ask customers to check a box to agree to receive offers and information. It's best to say you won't pass the details to third parties as you are likely to increase the sign up rate.

114 BUY IN A LIST.

For cold prospecting, it is possible to source external lists, and there are now many companies selling such lists. They must obviously consist of opted in email addresses. Not all lists are the same and measures of quality include the bounce rate (the percentage of emails that are undelivered). Ultimately however, it's the responsiveness of the list to your proposition that matters. A small list that products a 1% response is worth much more than a large list responding at 0.01%.

115 GET YOUR EMAIL DELIVERED.

Use a third party specialist else you may get your server or domain black-listed. If you use your normal site or ecommerce service for sending email then ask the following questions: does your supplier screen their customers to make sure they are not spamming as you will get tarred with the same brush if you are on the same sever; does your supplier have good working relationships with other ISPs; what procedures do they have to resolve delivery problems? Make sure that they obey the Sender Policy Framework (SPF). Remember that sending emails to invalid addresses will cause ISPs to flag you as a spammer – then none of their customers will hear from you again. If a domain that previously was good at receiving your email suddenly shows many email addresses as non-existent, then suspect you have been black-listed. However, note that 100% success suggest your emails are being discarded. Get in touch with the technical contacts at the domain to find out what is happening. Get the recipients who have not received your email shot to complain if possible. Slow down the email sending speed. Perform a deliverability audit – is the stuff actually getting through?

116 AVOID SPAM FILTERS.

Even after an email has arrived to a valid address, it can still be regarded as spam by the individual's own email application. The rules on spam filtering are constantly changing as the spammers try to avoid the rules and the suppliers try to catch them. For instance, putting "free" in the subject line or body of the email is a fair bet for getting filtered out. One good technique is to send some emails to friends, particularly if you haven't emailed that particular email address before, and see what gets filtered and what gets through. This is also good for checking what the email looks like.

117 GET YOUR EMAIL OPENED – THE SENDER.

Once your email has got through, the challenge is ensuring that your email is not deleted immediately by the target. Pay attention to the sender field as it is one of two pieces of information that the recipient will use to decide whether to open the email. It may be that putting your company name in will work best, or possibly just your first name. Results will depend on your target market and experimenting is well worth the effort.

118 GET YOUR EMAIL OPENED – THE SUBJECT LINE.

Make the subject line of interest by using personalisation whenever possible, for instance considering putting the target's name in the subject line as this has been reported as producing up to a 10% better response. Use relevant, snappy subject lines. Using money off special offers in emails is good, but avoid putting them in the subject line else the email will look like spam.

119 GET YOUR EMAIL OPENED – THE DAY OF WEEK AND TIME OF DAY.

Perhaps surprisingly, the day of the week and time of day has a material impact of the probability that your email is opened. This is probably because when a person opens their inbox and finds a big backlog of emails, they are more likely to delete emails without opening them. So get your message into inboxes at the optimum time – experiment to find out when that is for your market. Experience suggests that this will vary by country.

120 GET YOUR EMAIL CONTENT RIGHT.

Once you email is delivered and opened, you have a second or two to catch the reader. Fantastic creative absolutely does not guarantee success. For instance there's an issue around images versus text – remember that images are usually initially suppressed. The initial pane is likely to be one third the size of the web page – so take this into account. Don't require any scrolling to the right, scrolling down is OK. Most people look at the top of screen first, so you must hook them on the first part – this is where a logo may or may not be a good idea. A logo may be the only thing the recipient looks at. Don't forget that nowadays, many emails are opened on mobile devices. 85% of those are on Apple devices – so it's well worth testing on these devices. Around 50% of people say they will immediately close an email not optimised for mobile. Certain moods can be engendered by the use of certain colours and fonts so again test them to see what works best.

121 DON'T OVER-COMMUNICATE.

Sending either emails or a newsletter too frequently is counter-productive. If the perception you leave is that you are only interested in force-feeding more product, you will train your customers and prospects to ignore you, delete your emails, opt out or place you on a spam list. I myself experienced this from one store that sent me special offers every week after I bought. It was very irritating and I have never shopped there again.

122 COMMUNICATE INTELLIGENTLY.

Think about what you would like to receive and work hard to send what is relevant. The recipient's time is precious, so they must feel that they get more value from reading your communication than the time it costs them. Remember that if you put out an unsophisticated strong sales message this may destroy the implicit contract you have with the recipients and lead to more requests to unsubscribe. If you highlight something on your web site (always a good idea) then the recipient must be able to click through directly to the relevant page. Newsletters should keep to a common format just like newspapers do with TV times in a particular place – it makes you more familiar and hence more likely to be read. Track clicks on links if you can, that way you can measure the success or otherwise of campaigns.

123 KEEP TRYING.

Trial and error is needed to see what works with your prospects. One merchant reported that their most successful email campaign resulted from two lines of plain text while one longer email with images resulted in no orders at all. Use Google Analytics to check inbound traffic from marketing e-mail campaigns. You will be able to see exactly what style and layout works better for your customers from the results shown.

124 LEARN FROM THE BIG GUYS.

Subscribe to receive emails yourself and analyse incoming marketing emails in the light of the advice here. You will be able to glean best practice and see developing trends, effectively benefiting from the research and gurus employed by the big boys.

125 TRY TO GO VIRAL.

The rise of social networking has opened up new possibilities with email marketing. It's good practice to encourage people to forward emails to a friend or even add the contents of the email to their social network. These can be accomplished with links in the email.

126 MONITOR BOUNCE RATE.

Emails that can't be delivered are said to be "bounced" when you get notification that they have not been delivered. The bounce rate is a good measure of the quality of your email list.

127 MAKE IT EASY TO READ.

There are many email clients used to read emails. Check that your email is readable in as many as you can. The message here is that while a little work will reap major reward, the more environments you check, the more response that you will get. Make sure that your email can easily be read on the current crop of email readers and in the display sizes that are most prevalent. This changes regularly as new trends emerge, so is worth enquiring about this regularly. At the time of writing, it's worth considering how your email will display on a PC, Mac, Netbook, and on the free email services such as Yahoo, Gmail and Hotmail. Also consider varying from HTML to text to see what impact that this has.

128 BE DILIGENT IN MAINTAINING YOUR LIST.

Make sure that you remove email addresses that unsubscribe and that produce bounced emails. Be totally diligent about this. Collect more information over time from your customers and prospects, using a newsletter.

129 ALWAYS HAVE AN OBJECTIVE.

From each communication you should have one objective with an associated clear call to action. You need to make this absolutely clear and ideally it will be "above the fold" so people can readily see it. In some cases this will be to get a purchase there and then. In other cases you will simply want to move the prospect along the sales funnel. Any segmenting your email list you should aim to have the correct objective for the correct segment. Use Google Analytics to set up a goal to track each objective.

MARKETING YOUR WEBSITE

USE VIDEO

If a picture paints a thousand words then a video must need the entire dictionary. We all respond much better to visual prompting compared with text, and even better to moving images. After all, life is lived in video.

The video revolution has been enabled by cheaper, better equipment combined with ubiquitous faster download speeds. Video results in an ecommerce store that is much closer to being interactive by putting the consumer in charge. In addition, videos will help to keep people at your site, creating a rise in "stickiness".

Hosting video can be free. You can embed a video on your site but host it on YouTube. Another popular host is Vimeo. The often-cited disadvantage of hosting on third party sites is that it diverts traffic from your site, but this need not be the case. In contrast, it may be that people searching on these sites will find your video and come to your site as a result.

YouTube, Facebook and Vimeo will accept most video formats; once you've uploaded to these sites convert your video to a generic format that is pretty much available to everyone, eliminating the biggest technical challenge.

Videos can be used in conjunction with other marketing as a call to action, for instance by putting a link to a video in an email, and can potentially change other touch points into further marketing opportunities.

In addition, Google increases the rating of pages containing video – not surprisingly, given that they own YouTube.

With this all in mind, here are some tips on building online sales and improving customer relations using videos.

130 USE VIDEOS WHEREVER YOU CAN.

It has become very cheap to shoot and display videos on the web site. Showing products in use can be help tremendously in the decision to buy, so don't disappoint your customers.

131 GAIN ADDITIONAL PROSPECTS.

There's the potential for new prospects to find you after they see your videos on YouTube or other specialist sites. For this reason it's important both to embed your URL in the video and also to make it easy for viewers to forward a link to friends or other interested parties.

132 QUALIFY AHEAD OF THE SALES PROCESS.

Done right, a video can cause people who wouldn't have bought anyway to drop out earlier, thus avoiding wasted sales effort. Ensuring that people know what they are buying can reduce returns with an immediate positive impact on profitability.

133 SUPPORT YOUR SALES.

It's great to introduce your company, untangle complex ideas, explain products and show them in-situ using video. And the whole process will be generally more enjoyable for your prospects. A product demonstration showing exactly how problems are solved will sell where other media will fail.

134 EDUCATE YOUR CUSTOMERS.

Education can still have a surprisingly positive impact on sales. Hesitation arises from uncertainty. A customer who has had this uncertainty removed will be more confident and therefore more likely to make a decision. As the provider of the education you are likely to be trusted and to get the deal.

135 PRODUCE YOUR VIDEOS IN AN APPROPRIATE WAY.

One question is whether videos should be professionally produced or home-grown. This will be impacted by your size and budget and it's true that generally you get what you pay for. However, YouTube has made amateur footage more acceptable so with care (and a steady hand) you can produce a low budget video that still has business legs.

136 DON'T GO VIRAL FOR THE WRONG REASONS.

Although amateur footage is more acceptable on YouTube now, it's easy to make something that looks embarrassing. Embarrassing videos spread like wildfire on YouTube and social networks. Before uploading a video, make sure it's going to represent you in the way intended.

137 GET CASE STUDIES ONLINE.

Video case studies of customers recommending you generally produce a positive emotional response. A person explaining exactly how they were helped has more weight than any sales pitch.

138 SET OBJECTIVES.

Whichever approach you take, deciding what you are trying to achieve is critical. Then you need to plan the content - the subject, critical messages and how you will present them. These must all support your objective. So the questions to ask are whether you want to simply enhance the image of the business, provide technical information, help close the sale, or educate your prospects while cutting the number of calls. You decide.

139 MAKE THE PLAN SUPPORT THE OBJECTIVES.

Once you know what you are trying to achieve, it's time to act. You should be ruthless in limiting the length of the video, probably three minutes maximum. You also need to try to grab people in the first twenty seconds, so concentrate the most creativity on that part, and ensure you explain the benefits the viewer will gain. Remember that the image that YouTube will use will come from the first few frames, so try to make them relevant. You need to decide on the style – chatting, testimonial, demo etc. Make it interesting but relevant, e.g. someone who is highly photogenic may be a positive for some people, but a turn-off for others. You need to be consistent with your brand.

140 GET THE RIGHT EQUIPMENT.

If you are making your own video then the equipment list obviously includes a video camera, maybe a Flip as it is cheap or the latest iPhone as both are easy to use. Also important are lights and a good microphone, both of which will have a major impact on quality.

141 DECIDE WHO TO FILM.

To keep costs down ask staff or friends to audition and use those who do the best. Obviously if you have the budget, professional actors are likely to produce a more polished result.

142 EXECUTE EFFICIENTLY.

Then comes shooting, editing and the addition of a music track. If you want to do things yourself to save money rather than use a professional, then Movie Maker, pre-installed with Windows, is probably good enough to make a low cost video although iMovie, which comes with a Mac, is better. Be careful of copyright issues and remember that music can hinder as well as help. It may be worth spending the money on a professional voice-over, which you can find at www.voicebunny.com. You're not necessarily making a work of art but it must be both visually and audibly clear. Another possibility is to work with a local college. They have great equipment and students looking for experience and who have coursework assignments – there's a good chance that they can produce your video for free. It's not just videos; they may be able to help with other marketing materials too.

143 GET YOUR VIDEOS OUT THERE.

There's choice between hosting them on your own site, or on another web site with YouTube the clear favourite. If you use YouTube, you should establish your own dedicated channel in the form www.youtube.com/user/YourChannel. It's also possible to embed YouTube videos so that they can be viewed on your site. The good news about YouTube is that it provides the bandwidth for nothing and the speed is great, while solving the problem of which video format to use.

144 MAXIMISE TRAFFIC.

You can maximise traffic from YouTube itself by adding a title, keyword tags and descriptions to all of your videos. By mentioning and linking to your videos from blog posts, a Twitter feed and similar you can also help the rankings, and you should also link back to your own site from the YouTube description. Essentially the same guidelines to optimisation apply to YouTube as to Google generally. You can also use YouTube's Insight reports to find how traffic is finding your videos and then optimise around this.

145 EXPLORE VERTICAL SITES.

In some vertical markets there are also specialist sites showcasing videos relevant to your business, so it's well worth looking out for them too.

146 IMPROVE CUSTOMER SERVICE.

It's great to present product information by showing it in real life use. It will save mistakes in assembling and usage, improving service and reducing cost. Video can prove that a problem can be solved. If customers can find videos that enable them to solve their problem, you will both improve service and reduce costs.

MARKETING YOUR WEBSITE

MEASURE EVERYTHING

The image of a successful marketer has long been that of a sharp dresser, who is highly creative and absolutely makes their presence felt. Although there is some truth in this, and in particular creativity can be very important, behind every true marketing success story is a paranoid focus on figures. It's by measuring, improving and focusing on what works that fortunes are made. In fact, when you look behind any world-class success story in any field, including sport and entertainment, you will find a lot of hard work, attention to detail and measurement, as well as raw talent.

147 GET THE LATEST IDEAS ONLINE.

There are many forums online where ecommerce is discussed. While most have a large presence from suppliers who wish to promote their service, there will be many interesting discussions. Included in these will be discussions on measurement.

148 LOOK AT YOUR WEB TRAFFIC.

Your hosting service should provide you with statistics to see how many people visit, where they come from, what proportion immediately leave (bounce rates), what country they are browsing from and more. This information may also be available through an analytics packages.

149 USE GOOGLE ANALYTICS.

Google analytics is a free service from Google that allows you to analyse where prospects have come from and what they do when they arrive on your web site. A good ecommerce service will already have set this up and will make it available free of charge.

150 UNDERSTAND THE SOURCE OF TRAFFIC.

Using the analysis tools mentioned above it's possible to see where your traffic is originating. This enables you to understand which aspect of your marketing is yielding the most results and to then concentrate your firepower in that area. You can also look at the cost of activities in each area to determine which is the most effective.

151 USE GOOGLE WEBSITE OPTIMISER.

Google website optimiser is another free service from Google which allows you to test changes to the site and see what produces the best results. It's worth implementing this so you can test changes made to your site.

152 CONDUCT A/B EXPERIMENTS.

With Google Optimiser in place, you can now start conducting testing. This is usually known as A/B testing. You have two ways of presenting yours site, for instance A has a discount voucher field and B doesn't. You now compare results to see which results in the most orders. It's not at all unusual for people to be shocked by the results and to be able to substantially improve site sales as a consequence.

153 DETERMINE THE COST PER SALE.

The ultimate objective in measuring marketing spend is to see how many sales of what products result from each amount spent. This should be possible using Google Analytics. You then ramp up spend on the things that are working and focus improvements in the areas that aren't.

TOP TIPS **154–219**

EMBRACE SOCIAL MEDIA

I can still remember the first time that I saw the teenage daughter of a friend using Facebook, and it was only a few years ago. Since I joined, practically everyone I know has slowly but surely succumbed to the temptation too. Facebook has over a billion people using its service worldwide at least once every month. In fact, the last few years have seen a dramatic rise in all of the social networks – Facebook especially, but Twitter, LinkedIn, Google+ and also many others too.

As the number of people involved in social media has risen to astronomic heights there has been a tendency to believe that "everything is going social". This hasn't turned out to be true, and the fact that many people are involved in something doesn't automatically create an opportunity for every business. Billions of people walk every day, but that doesn't mean anything to your business unless you're selling shoes.

After making that statement, there are obvious challenges and opportunities for ecommerce firms in this area. In the sections below, we will try to identify just what these are and how to benefit from them.

In general, the challenge that social media presents is that your company and its offerings will almost certainly get discussed, and your detractors and competitors will almost certainly be present. If you aren't there, such discussion will be considerably more negative about you than if you were around to have an influence.

On the positive side, there is a chance of finding more customers from scratch and looking after the ones you already have better.

Probably the best opportunity to do this is simply making it very easy for your customers to recommend you to others. In the case of Facebook this will be their friends but in the case of Twitter this might be anyone interested in searching in your field.

Pretty much all social networks provide paid advertising, and if you have a very innovative and new product, this could be a major way of getting the word out. But in general there is a much bigger opportunity through search engine advertising, because that targets people who are actively looking for your products.

EMBRACE SOCIAL MEDIA

TIPS THAT APPLY TO MOST SOCIAL NETWORKS

These are the tips that we feel apply to all social media. There are also specific sections on Facebook and Twitter below, as these are the biggest and most important networks.

154 UNDERSTAND THE BENEFITS OF SOCIAL MEDIA.

The way you benefit from social media is when a) you attract new customers b) people who buy from you or like your offering share this with their friends or followers c) you diffuse criticism or customer complaints by providing customer service and other added value, and hence protect your reputation and grow customer loyalty.

155 BE THERE.

Many of your customers and huge numbers of your prospects are active on the social networks. Most of your competitors are too. You need to be there, if only to keep an eye on things.

156 LISTEN BEFORE YOU TALK.

Once you have found your customers then sit back and listen. Social networking is renowned for its real time opinions, use this to your advantage and use search engines to find people talking about you or your company. Unplug your keyboard and gather as much intelligence as you can, it often gives a fascinating insight. Even better take it a step further and look for your competitors' names, or search keywords that relate to your products or services. Never give up on listening, things are always changing and social networks can help to keep you ahead of the competition.

157 ELICIT ENGAGEMENT WHEN YOU SPEAK.

After locating people discussing your brand or the competition, start a dialogue with them. When you do decide to post content, make sure you ask questions and invite comments. Social networks are not a soapbox for one way traffic, that's a fast way to get ignored. So it is important not to comment too often and to try and add value when you say something. In particular avoid contributions which are simply intended to promote you and which stick out like a sore thumb. Try to develop a positive and professional persona.

158 PARTICIPATE POLITELY.

A person's online social space is sensitive; so respect it by being smart and polite. You wouldn't barge into a normal conversation with blatant advertising, and social networking is no different. Within my business, SellerDeck, we actively spend time trying to help customers participating on social networks. We direct people with queries to our online resources such as our knowledge base and online articles. Once you start, try not to give up. Make it part of your daily routine, schedule time to get involved in answering questions and engaging with others, it's very rewarding.

159 PRIORITISE FACEBOOK AND TWITTER.

You shouldn't worry about other social networks until you have cracked Facebook and Twitter, as these are by far the largest. That's why we have a list of tips for each of these networks.

160 SET UP PROFILES.

Although the priority is Facebook and Twitter, as well as setting up company profiles there (see tips later) also get a presence on Google+ and LinkedIn. Remember if you don't take the space for your company name, somebody else might. Try to tell interesting stories, maybe about how customers used your products in unusual ways. Avoid boring sales pitches and corporate flam. Ensure that your profile provides a great overview of who you are and what you sell. It must contain a link to your web site.

161 CONSIDER ADDING SHARING BUTTONS.

After your profile, one of the biggest and easiest ways to start interacting with social media is to add buttons to pages on your web site that allow customers to share things that they like. On each product page you can add interaction with Twitter, Facebook and maybe Google+, Pinterest and others if you wish. Like all editions, you need to assess whether the real estate taken on your web site is worth the benefit gained.

162 USE ADDTHIS.

AddThis provides useful code that enables you to add a series of social activities to your site embracing all of the main social networks. So consider it in your plans. Let people "like" both your site and individual products. AddThis will also provide information on how your customers are behaving. ShareThis is an alternative.

163 BE CREATIVE WHERE YOU PLACE YOUR SOCIAL NETWORKING BUTTONS.

Try to find clever places on your ecommerce store to put your social links. For instance, you might consider the order confirmation page where you could thank them for the order and suggest they share information with friends. You could do the same in the email that confirms the order. Be creative, maybe if you offer free shipping this would be a place to offer sharing?

164 PROVIDE COMPELLING REASONS TO VISIT YOUR SITE.

If you are promoting yourself on social networks, include discount vouchers, tips, special offers or competitions to encourage people to visit your site, just as you would with any other marketing. If these new customers are pleased with the result, they are likely to share with others. This is where you begin to get the real results of social networks.

165 PROMOTE YOURSELF, NOT THE SOCIAL NETWORK.

Most social networks commentator's talk as though the social networks are an end in themselves; they're not. Make sure you don't send traffic to social network sites that should be staying on your site and buying your products, rather than being exposed to the competition. So it's helpful for a customer to share their likes of your products with their friends, but probably not to join a social network from your site.

166 ALLOW REVIEWS TO BE SHARED.

If your customers can review your products, make sure these reviews can be shared across social networking sites, a really simply way to do this is through ShareThis and similar add-ons.

167 USE THE ANALYSIS TOOLS THAT ARE AVAILABLE.

Most social networks enable you to analyse traffic and there can be a wealth of interesting information available. Once you work out how your customers are sharing, you can modify your site design. You don't want to complicate your design for no reward, you may even reduce sales. Use URL shorteners like bit.ly whenever you post a link so that you can track how many people are clicking the link. Look at how effective different types of links are in various social networks. It might be that Twitter followers are interested in new developments while Facebook fans click on free coupons.

168 RESEARCH AND GET IDEAS.

Social Networks are brilliant for asking questions. The open nature of these communities allows anyone to ask, view or respond, so the potential is obvious. Thinking companies use these networks to gain insights into the market as well as broadcasting their own messages. So you can use social networks to identify people who influence others, see what is trending, check on the competition and understand better what your customers want. On the other hand, social networks can use up a huge amount of time. Researching the medium takes substantial effort, so make sure it's concentrated in the right place. Check your demographics and find out if your customers use social networks. If so, which ones? Talk to your customers and friends about which social networks they use, to try to not miss any new trends. After you have a presence on Facebook and Twitter, consider more options like Google+, LinkedIn, Instagram, and Pintrest. There are many more social networks and they are developing and changing all of the time.

169 THINK ABOUT THE DEMOGRAPHICS.

The links that people have on Facebook are most likely to be social and will cover many years, running back to school friends and relatives. These are people that the user may or may not have much in common with. In contrast, Twitter connections are more likely to be related to interests and LinkedIn to similar business activities. As a result, different networks will work best for different types of business.

170 THINK ABOUT THE AUDIENCE AND YOUR OFFERING.

Practical Ecommerce performed a survey among their readers and found that nearly 80 percent of readers got less than 5 percent of their sales from social media. 13 percent believed that they got between 5 to 10 percent from that source. Against this, Eventbrite, who market events in the US, found that Facebook was the top site for referring traffic, beating Google. Every customer that shared their purchase of an event with their friends on Facebook, led to 11 extra visits to the Eventbrite web site. Of course, attending events is a fundamentally more social activity than buying goods or services.

171 DON'T GIVE TOO MUCH AWAY.

Coupons providing discounts may be very popular, and "Social Media Gurus" are always advocating their use. But if all you are doing is giving away margin without getting additional business, that's bad news. So track what's happening and make your decisions based on business rational, not the advice of people with an axe to grind.

172 DON'T CONFUSE YOUR AUDIENCE.

Whenever you offer additional options, you run the risk of confusing and diverting customers. So it's important to ensure that all social media integration with your site provides a net gain, as the benefit may be outweighed by confusing your customers with too much choice. It is probably an idea to limit the use of such buttons and be very selective on which social networks you support. Testing different options and seeing how your audience responds is a good idea.

173 USE AUTOMATIC FEEDS.

It's a standard feature on Facebook to push out Tweets automatically to Twitter, and Twitter allows automated, scheduled publishing. There are also many other automation tools around such as Hootsuite and TweetDeck. Just be careful not to lose the personal touch and make sure that what you do is appropriate for each network.

174 WATCH THE LOAD TIMES.

Finally, make sure that your social tools load at the end of the page to avoid slowing down page load times. It may sound like a minor point, but the gains from social media could easily be offset by the loss due to slower pages.

EMBRACE SOCIAL MEDIA

GET MORE FROM FACEBOOK

These tips are specific to Facebook and should be read after considering the general tips for social media, all of which apply to Facebook.

Facebook's strategy appears to be to maximise the time people spend on their site by opening up their platform to third party developers and encouraging people to come to Facebook and then stay within their "walled garden". They are also extending the reach of Facebook across the web by allowing people to use their Facebook logon to access third party sites. As well as this, third parties can embed Facebook functionality in their sites which then feeds data back to the Facebook ecosystem.

In fact, Facebook seem to believe that the more time people spend on Facebook and the more information they can glean from their customers, the more they will be able to monetise this traffic and knowledge.

The centre of the Facebook universe is the Facebook account which is owned by an individual who must give their real name. People can then mutually decide to link up as "friends". Facebook is great at suggesting possible friends based on the network of existing friend's and most people find they are quickly connected to most people they have known for many years. So a friend usually replicates past or present real-life friendships.

Anyone can un-friend any existing friend. Facebook users can send any number of messages to their friends. Facebook also allows companies to have their own pages and Facebook users connect with these pages by "Liking" them.

Facebook lets you easily upload photos and "tag" them with the names of your friends. The result is that Facebook has become the biggest photo sharing site in the world. You can post what you've been up to and Facebook decides what information to put into each individual's newsfeed.

You can set up an "event" for a party or wedding and easily invite your friends. Basically, it takes social interaction and computerises it, mostly by making it easier to do what groups of humans have always done.
Here's a quick Facebook primer:

- Like. Any user of Facebook can "like" a company's Facebook page, as well as blogs, products and many other objects. The Like button can show the faces of friends who have already pressed it, so there is a potential multiplier effect. Pressing the button makes a connection to the publisher that persists. A proportion of Likes will show up on friend's news feeds (see below). According to Facebook this "gives positive feedback and connects you with things you care about". When you own a company Facebook page you can look at "Facebook Insights" which will tell you a lot of demographic information about the people who Liked the page. Facebook also uses the information about what people like for its own purposes and in a number of ways. Similar functions are "Recommend" which is self explanatory, and "Send" which provides the ability to send a message with a URL to friends through their wall or email address.
- Send. The Send button allows your audience to choose to send some of your content to their friends.
- Comments. The Comments facility lets users comment on any piece of content on your site.
- Share button. This is a legacy button, which is no longer going to be supported by Facebook. The Like and Send buttons have taken priority.
- News Feed. When people visit Facebook they see a constantly updated stream of information based on what their friends are doing. This shows pictures, what friends like, what they share and postings between the walls of user's friends.
- Wall and other communication. The Wall can be used for friends to post messages for each other and the Wall can be seen by anyone. This is designed for short immediate notes. Status updates allow users to create messages for their friends to read. The answer to the question "What's on your mind" is a status update. Friends can respond with comments or a Like. Photo tagging allows people to tag

photos with a brand, product, company or person's Facebook page. The poke feature allows people to attract the attention of their friends.

- Events, marketplaces, places and deals. These are all additional features used within Facebook. For instance events are things that are going to be happening e.g. weddings and parties, that allow arrangements to be made and memories gathered.
- Facebook Ads. Facebook allows you to pay to advertise as well as providing some free services. For the paid service, you have a lot of control over who sees the Ad e.g. age, sex, interests, and you only pay when someone clicks on the Ad. You can also "sponsor stories". This is a fast changing area as Facebook intend to make most of their revenue here.
- Social plugins. These enable web site owners to put the Like Button, Recommendations, Login and more on their sites. The capability to allow web site developers to get and send information from and to Facebook is known as the "Graph API".

That's all great, but the question is, can this be useful for an ecommerce business? In the following tips we explore the possibilities.

175 LISTEN TO REAL EXPERTS.

Michael Dell, founder of Dell Corporation, came up with an interesting quote. He said, "I think you'd be crazy not to be using social media, because it's the quintessential force of our time in terms of communicating with customers and sharing information. You can go out there and get your message across directly to lots of customers, lots of prospects." Michael Dell was an early advocate of selling across the web so his opinion is very interesting. Facebook wants to be the go-to resource when it comes to all things advertising and ecommerce, for businesses large and small... That's why many aspects of Facebook have been changed to help businesses use the platform.

176 DON'T OVER COMMIT.

All of the latest figures seem to show that while Facebook usage remains high in its most mature markets like the US and UK, and Facebook is still the world's biggest web site, time spent on the site in these markets is at best flat-lining. So keep an eye out for the trends.

177 UNDERSTAND THE PRINCIPLES OF FACEBOOK.

Facebook is about friendship that takes place on a relatively small scale. For individuals, in contrast to traditional communication tools, it's much easier to expand their network with relevant people, or communities based on mutual interests. As a result, these communities have brought much more influence to individuals and it potentially heralds a major shift of power from company to consumer. Although there are a huge number of total users, it is hard to make Facebook work for a businesses on a large scale. You can only engage with people on Facebook on a small personal scale. Something you do might go viral, but this has a frighteningly small probability. It is where lots social networking marketing advice is plain wrong. Most activities just don't scale. The business challenge is to address that issue.

178 ASSESS THE RELEVANCE OF FACEBOOK TO YOU.

Facebook is most relevant in the consumer or entertainment space. Selling to businesses is a different story. The family and friends of, say, a heating engineer aren't likely to be interested in the arcane details of heating systems. In contrast if you're in the entertainment business, the friends of your existing customers are much more likely to be prospects. If word of mouth is important in your field, Facebook could be a big factor. Facebook has the most potential for start-ups and small companies where a small advantage and a few extra customers is more significant. Having said that, large brands at least are going to be subject to discussion on Facebook, so it's good for them to be involved. Play.com stated that customers who came through Facebook placed 30% higher orders than the average, and this certainly gives food for thought. It is possible that Facebook may work best for ecommerce businesses if you have innovative new products that aren't well known or if you are the exclusive supplier of goods. In both cases raising general awareness will benefit you because all sales will actually come through you. The key is to remember the connected nature of social networks, recommendations prove to be the best type of sales lead and social networks can act like a mega phone for both praise and condemnation.

179 PARTICIPATE APPROPRIATELY.

You can only engage with people on Facebook by being interesting and interactive. To get the most from the medium, use "we" and "I" and take strong positions, either positive or negative. This last advice comes from published research by Dan Zarrella, which looked at ten thousand most liked Facebook pages, analysing more than a million posts. It just applies to Facebook, not necessarily to other social networks.

180 PROVIDE SERVICE.

Although we are principally looking at Facebook as a marketing channel, it has another benefit. If you monitor for any discussion of your company, you will find queries and also be able to pick up service issues before they are broadcast too widely and become a big problem. Helping with enquiries and problems boosts the perceptions of your brand and service.

181 SET UP A FACEBOOK PAGE.

The first action for any ecommerce business that wishes to avoid being out-flanked on Facebook is to set up a Facebook page for their company in the form www.facebook.com/mybusiness. And the good thing is that it's free. You should do this if only to stop someone else taking your name. One development of interest is that consumer brands now seem to be directing people to their Facebook pages in advertisements in preference to their own web site. However, it's hard to see that this is the right approach for an ecommerce business.

182 MAKE YOUR FACEBOOK PAGE USEFUL.

It's important to provide items of genuine interest on your page. Don't allow yourself to make too much of a sales pitch which will be counter-productive. Try to limit yourself to three useful posts to every self-serving one and ideally post regularly. You should decide on the tone that you want to set. Are you serious and reliable, or are you fun and lively? This will depend on the products you are selling and the demographic that you are targeting. However, don't try to be something that you're not. Ensure that you answer questions posted to your page. Consider putting Ads on your Facebook page, some companies have reported these can result in up to a 6% click through.

183 BUILD AN AUDIENCE FOR YOUR FACEBOOK PAGE.

You can build an audience by getting people to "Like" your Facebook page by clicking the Facebook Like button. This is a bit like agreeing to be friends, except that the initiative is entirely on their side. Apart from having an attractive page with interesting content, you can encourage people by offering exclusive content and only allowing people to post who have Liked you. Facebook says that the average person who presses "Like" has more than twice as many friends as the average and is generally more curious. The same group click on links to external web site more than five times as frequently. Fans won't ever revisit your page unless there is good reason, and that's just the way that they interact with their friends pages. It's important to realise that the more they visit, the more likely your postings will appear on their timelines reminding them of your existence and providing an opportunity for them to tell their friends. If when they arrive, it's dead space they will not bother coming again. Remember, don't post too much.

184 UNDERSTAND HOW YOU COMMUNICATE WITH YOUR FANS.

After people Like your company page, they become your "fans". You can use messaging capability to send broadcast emails to them. Alternatively, you can target them based on their gender, age and location. Whenever you post anything on your Facebook Page, it may appear in your Fans' news feeds, depending on Edgerank, discussed elsewhere. In fact Facebook has said that only 16% of company posts, on average, will appear in a fans news feed. Facebook says that the average user has around 250 friends, and if the user responds to your page or your posting, the item might appear in their friends Newsfeeds. If they then Like you, they are added to your fan base and their network of friends becomes potentially reachable. However, this multiplier effect will only happen if what you do is highly engaging.

185 UNDERSTAND HOW EDGE RANK AFFECTS VIRALITY.

Facebook calculates "Edgerank" in order to identify what actions to share on friends or fans timelines. The equation is: EdgeRank = Time Decay + Affinity + Weight. Time Decay is just about how fresh the content is. Something that is a week old is very unlikely to be seen by anyone. Affinity is a measure of how close a person is to your company page. If they visit it regularly, or comment on things that you post, they will be seen as closer. Similarly, friends that are always communicating with each other have a high affinity and each other's actions are more likely to be seen on each other's timelines. Finally, weight is about the effort of the action. A Like is just one click, so the weight is low. Uploading a picture or posting a long comment has a much higher weight (video would be even better) as it requires more action on a user's part. So if this morning you post a picture with a question, then someone who has visited your page several times in the last few days sees it on their news feed, comments on it and uploads a picture themselves, it is much more likely to appear in their friends news feeds. Just remember that "Chris Barling likes SellerDeck" and similar can be damaging if it continually turns up on a timeline. Instead of motivating your fans it will irritate them and they will Unlike you.

186 PUT THE LIKE BUTTON ON YOUR SITE.

Adding the Like button provides an opportunity to increase traffic and grow your number of Fans. Each click gives the potential for your site details to appear on the customer's friends Facebook news feeds. Consider adding "Like us on Facebook" to things such as your newsletter and the order confirmation page. The subtle problem is that as Facebook records all of your customer's likes and interests, competitors can target them through Facebook advertising.

187 USE THE INSIGHTS CAPABILITY.

Every Facebook Page comes with a free analytics capability called Facebook Insights. This gives information on the activity of people that have liked your page, and how much your page is being discussed. You also can see demographic information on the people that have liked the page including gender, country and age. This is a great start to profiling your customers and prospects, which can be used in subsequent marketing campaigns.

188 ENSURE YOU MONETISE YOUR FANS.

The only point of building your fan base is to get them to visit your ecommerce store and make purchases or to influence their friends to do the same. The big argument against Facebook ecommerce is that Facebook is all about socialising not shopping. Would you be happy for someone to try to sell you something while you were watching the match, eating in a restaurant or seeing the latest episode of your favourite soap? There is no way to broadcast to all Facebook users (although you can advertise, see later) so the argument is that selling is entirely counter to the culture, and is therefore hard. So although the objective of monetising your fans is clear, it must be approached carefully. You may get visits as a result of your general brand building, but you can also refer to special articles on your web site, announce new products on your Facebook page with a click-through link and provide discount vouchers. You need to make sure you are not significantly cannibalising existing sales with your activities or giving discounts to people that would have bought anyway.

189 UNDERSTAND THE PRINCIPLES OF ADS ON FACEBOOK.

BusinessWeek.com stated that banner advertisements on Facebook get only 20% of the number of clicks compared to other Ads on the web. Their other findings were that Google gets users to click on their first Ad 8% of the time. Facebook's users click only 0.04% of the time. There is however a positive way of looking at this. Since you can decide to only pay for clicks, this could be a cheap way of building your brand through advertising. Comparing Google with Facebook misses the point. Google searchers are thinking about a problem and looking for a solution. Facebook users aren't. It means that Google searchers are a lot closer to a purchase. That's good, but there are issues. If you have a unique or new product which no-one knows about, then Facebook may be much better. Capturing a person's interest at an earlier stage in the sales funnel may enable you to short circuit the competition, and may avoid head to head price comparison. It's very early days of advertising on Facebook, and no doubt further insights will emerge.

190 CONSIDER ADVERTISING ON FACEBOOK.

Facebook allows advertising, and in fact their plan is to make most of their money through this route. Your adverts are displayed when a prospect is viewing Facebook and you only pay when they click on your advert. Unlike Google, Facebook allows an image to be displayed with your advert. You can also pay for each impression but that almost certainly isn't the best option for ecommerce merchants, where pay-per-click is generally better. You make a bid on how much you wish to pay, and the higher your bid the more likely your Ad is to be displayed. Generally speaking, the proportion of people that both see your Ad and click on it will be small – think one in a thousand or much less. Google click through will be much higher as people are specifically searching for products on Google. However, the key metric is not the click through rate but the cost per conversion. As well as straight Ads, you should consider Sponsored Stories and Promoted Posts, which are discussed below.

191 CAREFULLY SELECT THE DEMOGRAPHICS FOR YOUR ADS.

Facebook allows you huge control over who will see your Ad. You can select the age range, sex, education, relationship status, location and interests. In other words, if you are selling Star Wars merchandise, you can just target people who are interested in Star Wars.

192 UNDERSTAND HOW VIRAL WORKS IN THE ADVERTISING SPACE.

Once we have built a substantial base of fans of our Facebook page (people that have "Liked" the page), there are options to both target those fans and their friends, as explained elsewhere. It's the fact that there is interesting content on the Facebook page that will cause people to Like the page and maybe tell their friends about it. It's when we have interesting posts that people Like those and maybe pass them on to their friends which is the viral effect. So it's making sure that content is interesting, engaging, and not spam that enables the viral quality of Facebook to be exploited.

193 CONSIDER LOCAL ADVERTISING.

Try to be very selective on how you advertise, and continually refine your targeting to reduce the cost of each lead and sale. Watch how the Facebook Ad Exchange develops where you bid for Ads. A great benefit of Facebook advertising is that you can target localities. So it's worth discovering if this can improve response rates, particularly if you have a significant presence in one area. Although ecommerce is national, people can still feel re-assured that they can visit you and get support, see products or make returns.

194 LOOK AT SPONSORED STORIES.

Sponsored Stories allow you to take a post on your Facebook page and pay to have it seen down the right hand side of people's Facebook pages. They can be targeted like an Ad and in most ways are identical to Ads. The exception is that they are displayed with engagement information showing likes, shares and comments. They are likely to be best at trying to build up the fan base of your page.

195 THINK ABOUT PROMOTED POSTS.

Promoted Posts allow you to get a post on your Facebook page to show up more widely in your fans news feeds than they otherwise would. You can optionally also target the friends of your fans. Unfortunately, Promoted Posts are only available to companies of between 400 to 100,000 fans. They are likely to be best at getting people to take a specific action such as visit your site, download a tips booklet or take advantage of an offer.

196 ASSESS FACEBOOK ADS VERSUS GOOGLE WEB ADS.

Although Facebook reaches more than half all Internet users, Google reaches ninety percent. Google has click through rates on adverts around the web of around 0.4%, Facebook 0.04%.

197 UNDERSTAND FACEBOOK VERSUS TWITTER.

Twitter may be better at making quick connections to a large number of people. If you want to communicate more complex messages accompanied by drawings, photographs and videos, Facebook may be a better option. Understand that Twitter is a "fire hose" where anyone that follows you gets 100% of your posts (if they are logged on to Twitter), while Facebook on average only passes on 16% of your posts to your fans. The biggest difference between the two is information degradation. With Facebook thanks to Edge rank your content is delivered to the most relevant people for longer.

198 WATCH OUT FOR FACEBOOK GIFTS.

Launched in the US in September 2012 Facebook Gifts makes buying gifts for friends incredibly easy. Based on the "Birthdays and Life Events" section, you can purchase a gift, and have it delivered to your friend in a Facebook bag while choosing to share a message privately or publicly with that friend when the order is placed. This, of course, means that you can purchase on your friends actual birthday, and tell them what it is and when it will arrive, even though physical delivery may be later. This could be a boon to those afflicted with last minute tendencies. Friends will even be able to secretly swap their gift if they don't like it!

199 ALLOW LOG IN USING FACEBOOK.

An area that Facebook can help you in engagement with customers is through logon at your site. It's possible to allow people to log on using their Facebook account and this obviously minimises a barrier to transacting with your site.

EMBRACE SOCIAL MEDIA

USE TWITTER

These tips are specific to Twitter and should be read after looking at the general tips for social media, all of which apply to Twitter.

It took Twitter just over three years to achieve one billion tweets, while that's the total every three days now. Nothing illustrates the significance of Twitter more than that. The brilliance of Twitter is that messages have to be kept short (140 characters maximum), so they don't take too long to write and they don't take long to read.

People use Twitter to discuss their interests, share information and find out what the latest happenings are. It's well known that Twitter users knew about the jet crashing into the Hudson river near New York some time before it made it onto the mainstream news. Everything is immediate and Twitter lets people discuss TV programmes while they are being broadcast. Here's a quick Twitter primer:

- Account. An individual has to set up a Twitter account, and an account for a company is no different from any other account.
- Tweet. An account can post a "Tweet" of up to 140 characters. Any other Twitter user can potentially see this.
- Follow. You can "Follow" any number of Twitter accounts. When you access your account, you will see a stream of tweets from the people that you follow.
- Followers. Any number of people can follow you. When they log into their accounts, they will see your tweets.
- Retweet. If you particularly like a Tweet that you see, or think it is particularly interesting, you can "Retweet" it. This causes it to be seen by your followers.

– Hashtag. You can precede a single made up word with a # symbol in a tweet to associate your tweet with a particular subject. People can search on Twitter and if they search on the Hashtag you use they will see your tweet. Anybody can invent hashtags for anything.

Here are some thoughts on how to use Twitter for an ecommerce business.

200 UNDESTAND TWITTER.

Across the Internet, there are many forums discussing various topics. The brilliance of Twitter is that it can morph to become a discussion on any topic at any time. It's supremely democratic, as anyone can start using a Hashtag in the form #HateManU or #LoveManU or similar. People can look for Tweets on that topic or post comments against that Hashtag. You can create one or more a Hashtags that clearly relate to your website. This establishes an association between your Tweet and your business. This is particularly true when you retweet or reply to a Tweet.

201 UNDERSTAND THE POTENTIAL OF TWITTER.

Twitter now has over 500 million active users, growing fast. As a result, there are many prospects for your business on Twitter. As an ecommerce business you cannot afford not to be where many of your existing and future customers are active. It's important to realise that Facebook and Twitter are very different platforms, and large numbers are much more active on one rather than the other. So don't just focus on Facebook because it has higher overall numbers.

202 DON'T BE TOO OPTIMISTIC.

While some people would make you believe the aim of Twitter is all about gaining followers, the truth is simpler than that, it's a tool for building relationships. You might produce something that truly goes viral or you turn out to be such a fantastic and interesting writer that you gain a huge number of followers. But by definition only a very small number of people can succeed at this, and if you do you can probably pursue a different career. In reality, very little has a true wow factor, so very little (relatively) gets passed on to friends.

203 TRY TWITTER.

Even if you decide that Twitter is irrelevant you need to be sure. The growth of Twitter has been so rapid that the certainties of one year have changed dramatically by the next. A Twitter account is free, and you should start by searching for your company and products and topics related to your store. The minimum that you should do is to create an account on Twitter for your company name. The danger is that if you don't somebody else will.

204 FOLLOW YOUR COMPETITORS.

Follow the competition, see what they are doing and try to pick up useful ideas from them. Learning before you participate is always the first rule of any interactive activity.

205 PROVIDE CUSTOMER SERVICE.

One of the major reasons to be on Twitter is to engage with customers when they ask questions, request customer service or complain about an aspect of your company. So make sure you respond in a timely fashion. You really don't want others answering on your behalf.

206 BUILD UP YOUR FOLLOWERS.

The more people that decide to follow you ("Followers"), the greater your reach on Twitter, and the more potential it has. So do everything to encourage followers. As well as providing service and answering questions, when you Tweet, do it sensitively and try to add real value. Don't encourage people to Unfollow you by posting rubbish that just clutters up their screens. Continuous and unsophisticated sales pitches particularly fall into this category. The tips below outline a number of additional ways to help increase your followers and get your Tweets Retweeted.

207 INITIALLY PROMOTE YOUR TWITTER ACCOUNT TO EXISTING CUSTOMERS.

If you promote your Twitter account, or your company account to existing customers, that will help to increase your followers, and done the right way will only pick up those of your customers that are already on Twitter.

208 BECOME A KNOWN EXPERT.

There will be discussions and questions around the products you sell and the field you operate in general; if you participate responsibly, people will be encouraged to follow you. Participate in the discussions about things that you sell by searching for relevant words and Hashtags. Provide genuinely helpful advice and you will get the chance to talk about your company, products and offerings. Done skilfully, your participation will lead to people asking for your advice on what to buy.

209 USE COMMON HASHTAGS IN YOUR TWEETS.

Find out the Hashtags that your customers are using and then publish relevant content with these included. Basic market profiling says you should find more prospects for your store this way.

210 MAKE TWEETS INTERESTING.

Your objectives is to attract attention, so take a poll, make an offer exclusive to Twitter or maybe pre-announce a general deal on Twitter, hold a contest and include stories about your followers in your Tweets where possible. Post a blog on your web site and post a Tweet pointing to the blog. It's important that you do more than just promote links to your website. Yes, you can use some Tweets to promote specific products. Your followers are quite likely to expect to hear about your offerings. This is one of the reasons they chose to follow you. But your links do not always need to point to a page on your website. Offering relevant links to other non-competitive sites such as news sites will help to establish a better relationship with your followers.

211 FOLLOW TRENDS AND TRY TO BE FRESH WHILE BEING CAREFUL.

Twitter provides a list of "trending topics" which are what is currently being talked about. You can participate in these conversations and it does provide the opportunity to get known more widely. However, beware, as it is open season and it is easy to get caught out and become the butt of jokes if you stretch the connection to trending topics too far. This is particularly dangerous as you are responding in real time, which means you have less opportunity to think through the implications of what you are posting.

212 USE TWITTER AS THE FIRST PLACE FOR NEW PRODUCT LAUNCHES.

Launching a new product happens at a point in time and then decays, so a "now" medium is required and Twitter fits the bill. Having launched on Twitter, you can follow this up rapidly with a full launch to all customers. On one hand you want to make a noise on Twitter, on the other you don't want to encourage existing loyal customers to get their information from you on Twitter, where they will be exposed to the competition, rather than on your web site or mailing list.

213 LEARN ABOUT YOUR FOLLOWERS.

The more you know about your followers and what they like, the more useful you can be to them, the more loyal they'll be to your brand and the more money you can make from them. You might find that your followers click a lot more on links to coupons versus links to product updates. Knowing what gets people to actually click a link means that you can tailor your messages to get the most impact from your social media efforts. For example, you might find that your followers click a lot more on links to coupons versus links to product updates.

214 RESPECT YOUR FOLLOWERS.

You need to reward those that take the trouble to follow you. Understand that giving back creates trust, which is crucial for your brand, so think of ways that you can be useful to your followers. Share news and tips that they'll find helpful. Ask their opinions and interact with them. Respond to queries and discussions on your business quickly. Follow them back and Retweet their Tweets, join in discussions without always appearing to be just promoting your own interests (although you are). This really provides a positive vibe to your followers who will increase, feel more positive and be more likely to retweet you. This amplifies your message as it ripples through the followers of your followers and is the whole point of the exercise.

215 ENCOURAGE TWITTER TO PROMOTE YOU.

By participating regularly and building up your followers, you make it more likely that Twitter will suggest to other people that they follow you.

216 USE PAID FOR PROMOTED ACCOUNTS.

When you pay to promote your account, it becomes much more likely that others will follow you. This is because your account will appear more often when Twitter is suggesting who people might like to follow, who is like them and when they search for accounts. You only pay for every follower who signs up. Be careful, as prices have started rising.

217 USE PAID FOR PROMOTED TWEETS.

When you pay to promote your Tweets, they will appear at the top of search results when people search and your Tweet matches, they will appear near the top of the timeline when people log in to view their timeline, and if you target "users like your followers" they will appear in the timelines of people who aren't following you but have similar interests to your followers. You will only be charged by Twitter when someone else retweets, replies to your Tweet, clicks or favourites your Promoted Tweet. This is known as the Cost-Per-Engagement (CPE) model. Twitter estimates that 3% - 5% of people who see the Tweet will engage. There are a variety of targeting options including geography and device (e.g. mobile versus desktop). An example of a very effective advertising campaign using this facility is illustrated by the Tweet: "Happy Valentine's Day!! Show some love for your Valentine with a #HeartShapedPizza. Order at http://bit.ly/ff0Oc0". This elicited a 34% response. Just beware however as prices are rising.

218 MONETISE YOUR FOLLOWERS.

Getting followers on Twitter is the start, but not the end, of your use of the medium for ecommerce. So use offers, free information or product announcements to drive traffic from Twitter to your ecommerce store, where followers and other users can make purchases. Ensure you use services like bit.ly and Google Analytics so you can see what is working and make sure that the reward justifies the effort. Just make sure you don't post too many deals which may result in people that would have bought anyway getting a discount.

219 SPEAK TO THE WORLD.

The social networks are international. If you have hopes of selling internationally then Twitter may be able to help for research and test marketing.

TOP TIPS **220–276**

SELLING

When a prospect arrives at your site, your marketing is done. Now is the time to maximise sales, and that starts from your home page. The key principle in selling is to remove all barriers to deciding to buy and then making the buying process simple. That needs to be the focus within your store.

Typically the reasons on which a decision to buy is based are deep in our subconscious mind. Even those of us who consider ourselves highly rational can be surprised to discover this fact, typically after we have made a purchase against our normal behaviour. The overwhelming majority of people will end up buying what we feel is right, rather than going through a checklist.

Remember that the more annoyed prospects become, the less likely they are to buy, as it will feel wrong, even when everything else is right. You can create annoyance by, for instance, making it hard to find critical information like when an order will ship and how much delivery will cost.

The journey that makes up a prospect's experience of a site consists of all of the links that they click. When they come to click each link, they will have an expectation that a particular question about a product, term or condition will be answered. Every time we fail to meet that expectation, we are reinforcing the feeling that this is the wrong place to buy.

SELLING

DO THE SIMPLE THINGS WELL

Have you ever felt a degree of cynicism when reading the latest, greatest idea for business? If you have, then we share a common emotion. New ideas can help businesses, but rarely to the extent claimed, and sometimes they even have a negative impact. In contrast, some of the best business results can come by going back to the basics. The latest ideas may sound exciting but it's important not to neglect the simple things that remain critical for success. For instance, you need to highlight key facts like how to buy, delivery costs, guarantees and other aspects of your proposition many times in the site – once is never enough for these things.

These suggestions come at the dull end of the spectrum, and certainly aren't exciting or new. However, if you are underperforming in any of the areas mentioned, they could collectively have a dramatic impact on orders. When considering where to expend precious time and resources, there's only one critical question to ask. What will this do to my sales?

220 MAKE THE SITE FAST.

Adobe, the people behind PDF files and more, have recently said that when selling online "improving speed can reduce abandonment rates by up to 41%". Google also reports that a 30% increase in page load speed results in a 30% increase in business. They have also categorically stated that a speedy site will rank better and obviously buyers like fast sites too. In our experience, moving our customers to faster hosting packages has seen traffic to the sites grow up to 50%. It's simple. If you want a successful web business it's a false economy to cut corners on hosting costs. Your ecommerce cart needs to be fast too. Load times can also be optimised by reducing the size of images and pages. You can use Google Analytics to see which pages need attention and make changes accordingly.

221 THINK GOOGLE.

When you provide a lot of information on your products, this also has major search engine benefits. Search engines love content and if the content is constantly evolving, they will rank you even better. People do see optimising their site for search engines as a bit of a black art, and they are partly right. SEO is covered elsewhere in more detail, but some of the simple basics are well worth saying more than once. When people search, they type a "keyword" or "key phrase"(collectively referred to as "keywords) into the search box. Identifying the most popular keywords for your product range is the most important step. You can find this out by taking a free trial with Wordtracker www.wordtracker.com. You can also identify keywords that are well-used, but have fewer than average relevant pages on the web. These are your best opportunities – they represent niches where there are plenty of potential customers, but not too much competition. As a simple example that illustrates the benefit of careful keyword analysis, there are numerous pages on Google listing content and adverts for "Flowers", but only three ads for "Bunch of roses". Tools such as Google search analyser (part of Adwords) can help identify unique search terms. Even if you're not planning to use a pay-per-click (PPC) scheme it's worth signing up as it will save a lot of time. Once you know your keywords, you should make sure these appear regularly on your site. The keywords should appear in text, product names, page names and titles, and even image names.

222 ANSWER ALL OF THE PROSPECT'S QUESTIONS.

It seems incredible to me how some online retailers miss sales by simply not providing enough information about products. Don't just have one small image of a bouquet, but allow visitors to zoom in. Include instructions and practical tips on every aspect of using the product. If you are selling flowers, perhaps have a page with details of all of the ranges of flowers that you sell covering their history and when they are at their best. The more information that you provide, the easier it is for them to buy, and indeed it's a way to encourage them to return. It's noticeable that the best online retailers have spent huge amounts of time on their descriptions and pictures of their products. It really works.

223 ACCEPT PAYPAL.

Some online shoppers have a balance in their PayPal account, especially if they have sold some old items on eBay, and it may be burning a hole in their pockets. That's why it's quite common for online stores that start accepting PayPal payments to see their sales increase by around 10%. This may vary depending on the typical demographic of your buyer, but if you don't already accept PayPal it's well worth the minimal effort to do so.

224 MAKE SURE PEOPLE TRUST YOU.

To buy a bouquet from your site, people must trust you. There are a number of ways of gaining that trust, and you may be able to come up with your own ideas. As a starter for 10 though, here are some thoughts. Provide your contact details throughout the site, including a telephone number and physical address (it's a legal requirement anyway). Promote confidence by responding fast to emails, and answering the telephone quickly and professionally. Display logos showing your membership of trade bodies such as the IMRG or FSB, and join at least one of the merchant accreditation schemes like ISIS or SafeBuy. A photograph of your staff or premises can also do wonders.

225 SIMPLIFY ADDRESS INPUT.

Asking customers to just type in their post code when checking out and then using software to look up the full address automatically not only streamlines the process, but also reduces the risk of cart abandonment. Because delivery addresses will be more accurate you will definitely reduce costs by having fewer failed deliveries. Your follow up mail shots will receive a similar benefit. Check out postcode lookup services from Postcode Anywhere (www.postcodeanywhere.co.uk) who work on a pay-as-you-go basis.

226 GIVE A BREAK ON CUSTOMER REGISTRATION.

Sometimes obvious points can be missed. We all know how annoying it is to have to remember lots of passwords and I resent being made to create another account on a site I'll use once. In fact I won't buy from a store that takes this tack, and I am sure I'm not alone. People don't know if they'll return to buy again before they complete their first order so why force them to register? Give them the option to register later.

227 UNDERSTAND THAT "FREE" CAN BACKFIRE.

Trying different changes to your site and measuring the results may be dull, but the two examples below illustrate that massive and unexpected gains can result from small changes. In one documented case sales doubled simply by removing the discount code field from the checkout. The verdict was that buyers without discount codes felt ripped off if they didn't have a code. In another case sign-ups increased by 200% after "Free trial" was changed to "See plans and pricing."

228 USE MULTIPLE NICHE SITES.

You can use multiple sites each addressing a segment of your overall market. This enables you to make the site more relevant to your audience and can also improve search engine rankings.

SELLING

MAXIMISE SALES WITH OPTIMAL PRODUCT PAGES

Product pages are prime selling space. It's most likely that the decision to buy or not will be made while the pages are being viewed. So give them the thought they deserve. Put yourself in the place of the buyer and ask yourself what they would like to see.

229 BE CRYSTAL CLEAR.

Provide clear information on the critical details such as price, delivery times and charges. If buyers have to hunt, some won't bother and a sale is lost.

230 SHOW RELATED ITEMS.

When a shopper is looking at a particular item, there are always other items that naturally relate together and which a buyer is likely to want to purchase at the same time. Make sure you meet this need.

231 HAVE A CLEAR CALL TO ACTION.

The aim of a product page is to sell what's on that page. In most cases, this means clicking on an add-to-cart button or a checkout button. For sophisticated and high price products the sale may involve encouraging them to call to discuss and place their order. Since this is the objective, these "calls to action" should be prominent on the page. I remain shocked at how difficult it is to find out how to add items to the cart and checkout on some sites.

232 CLEARLY SHOW THE STOCK POSITION.

There are a variety of business drivers that vary the way that each business handles stock levels and unavailability. The important thing is to be clear with customers and ensure that their expectations are met. Failing to do this will result in upset customers and lots of customer service calls, resulting in lost business and wasted time.

233 A PICTURE TELLS A THOUSAND WORDS.

Look at the Asos site. This is one of the most successful ecommerce retailers of recent years and the pictures are brilliant. If yours are too, you will reap the rewards.

234 PROVIDE CLEAR CLUES WHERE YOU ARE IN THE NAVIGATION.

It's important that browsers don't get lost in your online shop. Show clearly where people are, for instance by providing a "breadcrumb trail" that shows each section in the hierarchy above the current position.

235 DON'T SKIMP ON INFORMATION.

Provide full details of all products for sale, allowing for all of the information that is needed for a decision to be purchase to be made. Nothing is more off-putting than not knowing what you are buying or not being sure if it will work the way that you need it to. For instance, will it work with your 24-volt system? If you don't supply the information, your prospect will click away to someone who does. If not all of the necessary information can be accommodated on the page, provide links to even more information on another page.

236 USE VIDEOS WHEREVER YOU CAN.

See the section that covers videos. Some studies have suggested videos can increase conversion by 20%.

237 USE CUSTOMER PRODUCT REVIEWS.

Provide the opinions of other customers on the products that you are selling. This will help considerably in the buying decision. This is covered in more detail later.

SELLING

TIPS FOR TURNING BROWSERS INTO BUYERS

Selling successfully to people who browse on the Internet has many of the elements of ordinary sales and marketing, but there are some subtle differences. For a start, the demographics of people who shop on the web can be different from those who shop in the high street, unless you happen to be selling hi-tech equipment or gadgets. Then there are the limitations of the medium. The Internet is good for products where you can make a judgment based upon sight or sound, but less good where smell, taste or touch matter. If you need more than sight or sound then you will have to build trust – customers will need to have confidence that fruit will be ripe, clothes will fit and so on. You can build trust by establishing a reputation, and by reducing the risk to the buyer by offering a truly no-quibble returns policy.

The key to sales is offering what the customer wants, at a price they are happy to pay. In your e-store, the buyer cannot easily ask questions of you, so you need to provide all the information they require to make a decision. It is very easy to drive someone away on the web – the world is only a click away – so minimise the barriers to buying.

Remember, once they have arrived at your web site, the marketing has finished and the selling begins.

238 DO NOT ASK THEM TO LOG IN OR SUPPLY ANY DETAILS BEFORE THEY CAN LOOK AT YOUR PRODUCTS.

There will be plenty of time to get their name and address once they have decided to buy something. It is nice to offer regular customers some form of recognition, like showing their name, but if you ask for it too early, it's like an over-familiar salesman. Most buyers will leave your site rather than fill in a form. Your job is to eliminate everything that gets in the way of making a sale.

239 DO NOT USE FLASH, OVERLY LARGE IMAGES, FRONT-DOORS OR OTHER GIMMICKS.

If you really need a short introduction, then at least have the grace to offer a 'Skip intro' link. Otherwise, 80-90% of your visitors will leave without opening the door. The rest will watch the animation and then leave. Ask yourself – do I need to impress technically, or to sell something?

240 MAKE IT EASY TO FIND YOUR PRODUCTS AND SERVICES.

If you have a home page, have a clear link such as 'Shop Here'. Clarity is key and particularly avoid flashing images or loud audio – everyone will assume that the rest of the site will give them migraines, and anyone shopping from work will be embarrassed.

241 MAKE IT EASY TO RECOGNISE WHAT IT IS THAT YOU SELL.

Have pictures of the sort of products that you sell in each category – some of your buyers may not speak your language, but they know what they want to buy. If you sell branded goods, use the brand logos (get permission) to reinforce your credibility and to speed people through. Link logos to the relevant sales section.

242 PROVIDE GOOD SEARCHING.

Bad search kills sales. The two problems are no results and too many or irrelevant results. Use a thesaurus to help – is it a boat or a ship, or a yacht? Use email, live chat and pop ups to try to salvage failed searches. Make sure that searching is fast and accurate, and provide searching on alternate information such as price range, colour or manufacturer. Create a drop-down list of the common attributes of your products to supplement your normal keyword searching. If someone is looking for a four-door car on your site, they don't want to have to guess if you called it 'four-door', '4-door', '4dr' or something else. The sales process should enable your customer to find the product most appropriate for them, and having found it, to buy it. Search is an important part of this process.

243 KEEP YOUR SITE UP TO DATE.

If you have goods that go out of stock, take them off the site or mark them as 'temporarily out-of-stock'. Make sure that your terms and conditions explain what happens if items do run out of stock. The Internet is very good at disposing of 'dead stock' at discount prices, but keep this in a separate section from your regular items so that you can update it easily. If you have any fixed-term offers, take them down as soon as they have expired.

244 HAVE SPECIAL PRICES AND YOUR FASTEST MOVING GOODS ON YOUR ENTRY PAGE.

Nothing succeeds like success. You need to grab customers and start taking their orders at the earliest possible point. Your top sellers and best offers will always have the greatest appeal.

245 OFFER TO KEEP THE NAME AND ADDRESS OF BUYERS – YOU CAN USE A COOKIE ON THEIR BROWSER TO AVOID SECURITY ISSUES.

This will allow your customers to checkout without having to type all their details in again. They will appreciate it, it doesn't involve yet another password and it's an incentive to shop again; do make it clear that a cookie is being used, however, and give them the option not to store it - after all, they might be in an Internet café or library.

246 MAKE YOUR PROMISES AND GUARANTEES CLEAR AND UNEQUIVOCAL.

Include them within the checkout process, even if they appear elsewhere on the web site. You need to inspire confidence in buyers who have never met you. If you ever have an issue, just make the refund – unhappy customers tell many more people than happy ones do, and will also waste lots of your time.

247 IF POSSIBLE, PROVIDE WAYS THAT CUSTOMERS CAN ASK FOR MORE INFORMATION,

and make sure that you respond in a timely manner. For instance, you might encourage them to email you questions. Alternatively, you might provide a telephone hotline, or enable an instant messaging service to that they can chat in real time while looking at your store.

SELLING

TIPS TO AVOID ABANDONED SHOPPING CARTS

Abandoned shopping carts aren't necessarily negative. Visitors quit their carts for many reasons. They may be competitors checking out your site, or consumers comparing prices and finding out your trading policies. Equally, customers may use your site and then place the order by telephone.

On the other hand, shoppers may quit because they find your checkout too complicated, or because they can't find a next-day delivery option. The following tips will help you minimise unnecessary abandonment, and encourage consumers to complete their purchase and to buy again.

248 MOST IMPORTANTLY, BUILD TRUST AND MORE TRUST.

Provide your contact details throughout the site, including a telephone number and physical address. Promote confidence, respond quickly to emails, and answer the telephone professionally. Independent customer feedback is looked at later – this can be a great trust builder too.

249 KEEP YOUR SITE SIMPLE AND EASY TO USE.

Divide the site into logical sections, with clear navigation links and a link to the home page on every page of the site. People generally expect navigation links at the top, left and optionally bottom of the page. Give full information with each product and provide a good search facility. Make sure that customers can get from home page to the 'Buy now' button in the minimum number of mouse clicks.

250 COMMUNICATE YOUR SHIPPING COSTS EARLY IN THE TRANSACTION.

Everyone hates surprises on cost. If the customer proceeds to checkout and decides the postage is too expensive, you have lost the sale. However, to justify a single postage charge, a customer may buy more than one product.

251 EXPLAIN YOUR GUARANTEE AND RETURNS POLICY.

A rock solid guarantee goes a long way to persuading people to buy. You must explain the distance selling regulations 7 day right of return in any case, so why not make this a strong selling point? Note that if you do not inform customers of their right, their rights are automatically increased by law.

252 DESCRIBE YOUR TERMS AND CONDITIONS.

When people can't find information, they tend to assume the worst. Go out of your way to provide comprehensive buyer friendly information. Make your site one that you would like to buy from.

253 EXPLAIN YOUR PRIVACY POLICY.

Provide a clear statement about how customer's data will and won't be used. A clear statement that customer data will not be passed to third parties except to complete the order process will help a lot.

254 EXPLAIN YOUR SECURITY AND ENCRYPTION PROCESS.

The best way is to use a Payment Service Provider (PSP), which will have gone through rigorous certification process. You can then state that no card data will be stored on your site. You can also purchase a security certificate (SSL Certificate) for your site and which will give you the golden padlock when people check out. Your ISP or web host can advise you how to set this up.

255 KEEP YOUR CHECKOUT PAGE UNCLUTTERED.

Any good web designer worth their salt will tell you that an uncluttered checkout will yield higher conversions. The more temptation the customer has to click away from the page, the more likely they are to do so. Use Google Analytics to examine the performance of your exit page. Trial a more uncluttered and focused checkout for a month and compare your results.

256 CATEGORISE YOUR SITE CONTENT INTO ATTRACTORS (WHAT PEOPLE LIKE) AND DETRACTORS.

For your own planning purposes, try to minimise detractors (ad pop-ups, need to register before buying and so on) and at worst balance them with attractors.

257 EXPERIMENT.

Different site layouts and options can have dramatic and unexpected impact on sales. For instance, one site reported a 20% increase in revenue after they added PayPal as a payment option. Another reported a 50% reduction after they prominently added the ability to input a voucher during checkout. People who did not have vouchers were obviously put off. Experimenting is important because each site will have slightly different visitor demographics – meaning that the people who visit different sites will behave differently. So you need to do your own trials.

258 REMEMBER CUSTOMER SERVICE IS KEY.

Encourage repeat business by going out of your way to meet customer needs. A happy customer will tell his friends, but an unhappy one will tell anybody who will listen.

259 BE AVAILABLE.

If customers cannot find out what they want to know from your site, they may try to get in touch with you. If they are unsuccessful, they will expect the same difficulty if they ever have a problem with an order – and they will go elsewhere.

260 ANALYSE YOUR SALES FUNNEL.

Look at every step in the process from arriving at your site to completing the checkout. Understand where people are dropping out and brainstorm ideas for correcting the problem. Then test alternative approaches and measure again so you can retain what works.

SELLING

TIPS TO RECOVER ABANDONED CARTS

If someone has abandoned a shopping cart in your store, it may still be possible to recover the order. These tips look at some of the techniques to achieve this.

261 MARKET TO ABANDONED CARTS.

If your ecommerce solution can support this, contact people who have supplied their details and then abandoned their carts. There can be many reasons why people have abandoned their order, including technical problems, running out of time, or issues of trust. Many businesses have found that this strategy can lead to significant increases in order volume. Contact can be by phone or email, and may involve an incentive to complete the order.

262 AUTOMATE MARKETING TO ABANDONED CARTS.

If you can automate marketing to abandoned carts, you will be able to do it consistently, which will lead to maximising what can be achieved.

63 COMMUNICATE THREE TIMES BY EMAIL.

Studies have suggested that maximum recovery will be achieved with three attempts to recover the order, with 60% of the recoveries coming from the second and third emails. We recommend you send emails after the cart has been abandoned after 1 hour, then another 24 hours and then another 48 hours. Just monitor the results and make sure that you are not having a negative impact by annoying customers or prospects too much.

264 OFFER A DISCOUNT.

In your abandonment email, offer 5% off in the first two emails and then 10% off in the final email. Obviously exactly what you can offer may depend on your margins and you should only do what makes sense from a profit perspective, bearing in mind that you have already borne the marketing cost.

265 THINK CAREFULLY ABOUT THE HEADING AND WORDING.

In the emails, make the first subject line one that suggest they haven't got around to finishing the order e.g. "Your shopping cart reminder". In the second maybe mention the discount and make the third the "Final chance to complete your order".

SELLING

TIPS FOR PRICING AND PROMOTION

It's much easier to carry out marketing activities in an online store than in a physical store – there are no labels to put out and everything can be automated. The well established ecommerce packages provide a bewildering array of marketing features, but it's important to get the business framework sorted out first. These tips are aimed at helping to do just that.

In fact, getting your average order value up is a crucial component of moving your business from good to great. At the same time, you can grow customer loyalty, as long as you give them a good experience.

266 ALWAYS OFFER MORE FOR SLIGHTLY MORE MONEY.

Never discount something that a lot of people will buy anyway, it is just giving money away unnecessarily. Offer them a great deal if they buy something else at the same time. This will please them and encourage them to come back, and it will increase the value of each sale that you make.

267 PROVIDE THE ABILITY TO BUY ACCESSORIES -

for instance batteries with a hand held GPS, paper and toner with printers and so on. They have to buy those things anyway, so try to make sure they buy them from you.

268 USE VOUCHERS OR COUPONS.

A person with a voucher or coupon feels that they have a special deal. It also ties them in to buying from you, because they cannot redeem your vouchers anywhere else.

269 EMAIL ELECTRONIC COUPONS,

so that they are exclusive to your email group. That way you reward your loyal customers without losing out on potential revenue from one-time buyers.

270 UNDERSTAND HOW CUSTOMERS BEHAVE IN YOUR MARKET,

as that will determine which tactics will work. Watch the trends in pricing and promotions among your competitors and in related markets. Learn from them, try things out, and see what works.

271 TRY TO FIND WAYS OF REDUCING THE PRICE FOR THOSE WHO ARE VERY PRICE CONSCIOUS, AT A COST TO THEM.

Airlines do this by discounting seats booked way in advance and sometimes at the very last minute, both of which are less convenient and popular than booking a few weeks in advance. You might do this by discounting returned goods or end-of-lines. Provided that it's not loss making, it's better to sell to price conscious customers at a discount than to lose the business to the competition.

272 GET CUSTOMERS TO RETURN TO YOUR ONLINE STORE

by analysing their sales patterns and making a special offer if they haven't come for a while. The section on email marketing can be consulted for more ideas.

273 IF YOU MAKE A SPECIAL OFFER, MAKE SURE THAT IT REALLY IS SPECIAL.

Have you been put off by companies that say that something is special, but it's hardly worth having? Or by offers made under a "loyalty scheme" - and badge it as such - that turn out to be the same as offers being made to everyone else?

274 ANALYSE THE VALUE OF YOUR OFFERING TO CUSTOMERS

and make sure the actual value (to a business) or perceived value (to consumers) exceeds what you will charge them. Otherwise you will always be trying to sweep water uphill.

275 DON'T UNDER-PRICE.

The quickest way that you can destroy a business is to engage in a price war where no one makes any money. Make your offering the best overall value, not necessarily the cheapest - unless you have clear cost advantages which mean that you can sell low and still make a good profit.

276 UPSELL IN YOUR CART AND AFTER THEY HAVE ORDERED.

Once people have placed items in the cart, offer further items at a discount. You could offer the extra items post-free as an incentive; you may want to identify your best selling lines, or to look at linkages between items (e.g. batteries with toys or a case with a laptop). With good software, you can do this easily. A customer who has just decided to buy is generally feeling favourable towards you – so it's an ideal time to sell them something else. Alternatively you could contact the customer post-sale to check everything is OK and to suggest some more possibilities. This gives a personal touch to your operation as well as generating additional revenue. However, beware as sometimes distracting buyers during the buying process can actually reduce sales. So any changes should be tested before the decision is taken to make any permanent changes.

TOP TIPS **276–337**

OPERATIONS

Operations isn't just about ticking some boxes at minimum cost, customer experience is utterly key. What is it like to have a query? What is it like to place an order? What if there is a problem? Look at everything from the customer's point of view. Then design systems and processes, and people policies, around the objectives that you wish to meet. If you want every customer to be given Rolls-Royce service, you must have a pretty pleasant environment for your staff. If they are treated badly, they will hardly treat your customers well. Be close to your customers and know what they are thinking. Always be prepared to take calls from customers, even when they are angry. It's an opportunity to learn.

In these sections we try to bear these principles in mind, while aiming to deliver the best service for the lowest cost.

OPERATIONS

CONSIDERATIONS FOR SHIPPING AND DISTRIBUTION

People who buy in a hurry expect the goods to be delivered in a hurry too. This is no problem for digital products like music, software and images where delivery can be made electronically. It's harder when you have physical goods to be shipped to the customer. Distribution is an area where bricks and mortar companies may even have an edge. If you already have a warehouse and make mail-order sales, then you are better placed than a start-up company that only has a web site.

As a merchant, you need to be clear with your customers what you offer and then live by it. If you outsource, be aware that you can't outsource responsibility. Buyers don't care why you have failed or whose fault it is – all they care about is getting what they have paid for. And if you or any of your staff ever tell your customer that a delivery problem is their fault because they didn't read the small print, this will guarantee that they will never buy from you again, and will tell their friends likewise

So here tips for making a success of your distribution.

277 BE AHEAD OF THE GAME.

Make sure that you are appropriately resourced for expected demand. For many companies this involves seasonal planning but you also need to gear stock levels and the warehouse for promotions if they are likely to produce a big response.

278 MANAGE CUSTOMER EXPECTATIONS.

Every customer wants answers to two questions about delivery – what does it cost and how long does it take? You must clearly answer these questions, preferably on the home page, with links from every other page. You must also be clear about the options – do you offer expedited/next day delivery? A specific timeslot or a weekend delivery? Do you deliver to a work place or offer gift wrapping and messaging? Are there any special conditions e.g. you need a signature, you can deliver "round the back" or "To the neighbour on the left, looking at the house", can I track the delivery online? Amazon tell you that a book 'normally ships in 2-3 days' so you aren't too upset if it takes four. If you offer '24 hour delivery' then when do the 24 hours start? What are the time constraints, e.g. 'Orders received by 4pm normally ship the same day'.

279 DON'T BE PASSIVE.

Pro-actively check on the status of deliveries so you know about problems first and you tell the customer if delivery commitments won't be met. Provide helpful support for failed, late or attempted deliveries. Monitor customer satisfaction with delivery.

280 EXPERIMENT ON DELIVERY PRICING.

Experiment with the balance between delivery charges and product cost – try to encourage larger orders.

281 NO SURPRISES FOR THE CUSTOMER.

Make sure that you calculate shipping charges as part of the whole deal. You may need to charge by weight, by volume or by value of order. If you offer free shipping on orders over a certain value, make it clear whether that value includes tax. Clearly notify any delivery terms and conditions e.g. where you can't deliver, times you can't deliver.

282 MAKE ALLOWANCE FOR BACK ORDERS.

Back orders are a fact of life if you accept fax or mail-orders, so expect them in Internet selling too. Allow the buyer the choice of waiting for a complete shipment or taking part orders. Only charge shipping once – it is irritating being charged extra shipping when it is the merchant's fault that the item was not in stock. If this can't work economically, cancel back orders and inform the customer. Make it clear on the site how you will deal with these sorts of situations.

283 GIVE PLENTY OF FEEDBACK.

Placing an Internet order may feel risky for the buyer. Make sure your buyers are told that you have received their order, and keep them up to date with its progress. If you have to make a back-order, let the buyer know when the rest of the order is expected.

284 BE PRACTICAL.

Pick a reliable carrier. There are lots of carriers and they compete heavily. Value reliability over price. A lost buyer will probably cost you more than the difference in shipping cost. Pick a carrier that can track goods online. Give the tracking reference to your customer as part of the order processing feedback. Monitor the performance of your carriers. Ensure your postcodes are accurate to help carriers to perform. Be PAF accurate on labels. The label should carry any delivery advice e.g. "Leave around back", supplied by the buyer.

285 BE CLEAR ABOUT RETURNS AND GUARANTEES.

Sadly, some of your sales will come back to you. Some may be your fault but others may be beyond your control. Publish your returns policy and include it as part of the ordering process at the web site. Be clear in your terms and conditions about who will pay for return carriage. By default, it will be you and if it is, make sure your carrier can collect.

286 SAY WHAT YOU MEAN AND MEAN WHAT YOU SAY.

Don't over-promise. Repeat customers are much more valuable than one-offs. Make it clear when you will deliver and then stick to it – even if it costs you more. Customers appreciate merchants who go out of their way to meet their commitments.

287 SELLING OVERSEAS.

There are all sorts of pitfalls to exporting. Who is responsible for any duty or taxes on the goods? In Europe, the EU Directive on Distance Selling sets out a legal framework for shipping within the EU. The good news is that shipments within the EU are free of duty. In the US, Congress banned new Internet taxes - but government policy can change. Most large carriers can collect duty on goods when they arrive, but you need to be clear about who is going to pick up the tab. Generally it is the buyer's responsibility. Make sure they know. If it comes as a surprise to them when the goods are delivered, you are the one they will blame. There is a whole section later on international orders.

288 WILL YOUR CUSTOMER BE IN WHEN IT ARRIVES?

Customers usually have to go to work, so there may be problems in receiving your goods. Some companies are experimenting with deliveries to workplaces or to known drop-off points like petrol service stations. If you can offer this, make sure that you can deal with goods that 'go missing' en-route. Another approach is to offer delivery within more precise time periods.

289 CAN YOU OUTSOURCE IT ALL?

Outsourcing fulfilment can be attractive – letting a warehousing company store and ship the goods. Make sure it is clear who bears the risk of stock in the warehouse, both for fire and theft. If the warehouse contents vanish, who is left with the bill? If rats nibble your books, who pays? Check that you are properly insured if it's your risk. Insure it anyway if it's theirs – who knows if they have paid their premiums? Check on their performance – it is your reputation at stake.

290 PLAN YOUR RETURNS PROCESS APPROPRIATELY.

Depending on the nature of your business, you will have a higher or lower rate of returns. For instance, it's not unknown for clothing suppliers to face a 35% return rate. Depending on this factor, the cost of shipping goods relative to product cost, and what your overall proposition is, you may wish to make it incredibly easy to return goods in order to reduce your customer service cost. Or alternatively you may elect for a straight-forward and fair system. Remember though that people returning goods are generally unhappy and can easily cost a lot of money. There can be many reasons for a change of mind including wrong product, damaged or defective goods, not what was expected, not fitting or simply a change of mind. Your returns process should be planned appropriately. Obviously, your statutory obligations under the distance selling directive must be met.

291 MAKE RETURNS EFFICIENT.

Remember every contact with the customer costs money. Possible approaches are to send a "returns ticket" with the order making it easy for the customer to return or substitute goods, asking the customer to register returns on the website or deciding if it's cheaper not to return goods and just refund them, especially if the claim is that they are damaged. Obviously this needs close monitoring for fraud. The steps in the returns process are initial contact and returns authorisation, physically getting goods back, processing the return, making an appropriate refund, placing goods back into stock or quarantine, replacing goods and retaining the sale. If you are a multi-channel business you may decide to allow returns through any channel. Remember that returns to a store provide the opportunity to sell a replacement, while potentially creating further logistics issues. Returns by courier may be difficult to track and by post impossible. It's also worth considering that if the returns process is too easy people may exploit it, if it is too hard people will resent and it may end up costing more. Finally, ensure that once returns have been received you deal with the efficiently and quickly. You need procedure to make sure if they go back into stock, are returned to suppliers if faulty, are scrapped, are sold at a discount price or are refurbished as quickly as possible.

292 AVOID SERIAL RETURNERS.

One company had a customer who always ordered at least two dresses of different sizes and then returned one. This was great for them but terrible business for the merchant. If you get someone to who does this it may be better to refuse their orders. Anti-fraud systems may also help as someone with a refund for every order is likely to be flagged as a potential fraudster.

293 REPORT ON RETURNS.

Monitor the returns process as this can be expensive. There's not only the cost of processing and delivering the original order, there's the service time spent on the return and the cost of re-processing or discarding returned goods. It's a good idea to report Distance Selling Regulations (DSR) returns, no quibble guarantee returns, faults in goods, errors in despatch or fulfilment, change of mind returns but always ask for a reason for the return, it didn't fit, description wasn't accurate etc. Check if certain items are returned more frequently as you may need to drop these or discuss with them with the supplier. You may also find that improved packaging of outgoing and returned goods can make a big difference to numbers of returns and the likelihood of being able to put them back into stock.

OPERATIONS

TIPS TO MINIMISE YOUR LOSSES FROM FRAUD

There's a mighty battle going on between web stores and fraudsters. In the US, fraud is now several billion dollars per annum according to CyberSource. The good news is that after years where the scamsters had the upper hand, merchants are slowly starting to win the war.

It's important not to just reject all orders that look suspicious, but to get a balance between fraud prevention and losing good business. You are not just at risk from fraud, you are at risk of losing good business from over-zealous anti-fraud measures. It's also crucial to remember that fraud varies greatly between different product sectors. For example, most of us would instinctively know that fraud is a problem when selling unblocked smart phones. However, I have known merchants selling bibles and model trains to suffer as well. Assumptions can be dangerous. These tips are based on a range of real life experiences and should make sure you stay on top in the battle against fraud.

294 USE THE STANDARD BANK ANTI FRAUD MEASURES.

The good news is that the banks have started to take online fraud seriously. They now offer a range of services such as address verification (AVS) that checks the billing address; CV2 (the code on the back of the card), which endeavours to determine that the buyer has access to the physical card; and 3D Secure (also known as Verified by Visa and Mastercard SecureCode), which requires a password. When 3D Secure is used, the banks are prepared to guarantee the payment if the buyer claims they didn't carry out the transaction.

295 INSIST ON DELIVERY TO THE CARDHOLDERS ADDRESS.

You can choose to not allow delivery to an address other than the cardholder's. This will reduce fraud, but at the cost of lost business. You will loose sales where one person is buying on behalf of another, or sending a gift. You will also lose orders from people who are in full time work and want their deliveries made to their work addresses.

296 MAKE SURE YOU ARE PCI DSS COMPLIANT.

The widely disliked Payment Card Industry Data Security Standard (PCI DSS) has also been introduced to make it more difficult for scamsters to acquire big treasure troves of card data. Any organisation processing payment cards must adhere to its rules or suffer fines and/or loss of processing facilities. The easiest way to comply for a small trader is to use a payment service provider like WorldPay or PayPal. We support this standard, even though it appears to place obstacles in the way of merchants. We have seen a big rise in organised and highly intelligent hacking attempts. It's vital that legitimate businesses fight back by raising the bar as high as possible.

297 USE A SPECIALIST ANTI-FRAUD SERVICES.

Alongside the bank-based initiatives, there has also been the rise of independent anti-fraud services like Datacash Fraud Services, which now checks more than 20 million online payments a month, claiming to detect around 97% of all fraud. I must declare an interest here as my company, SellerDeck, has integrated The 3rd Man into its own payments service. The many elements that the anti-fraud services look at including IP address, electoral roll and spending patterns across cards, buyers and addresses. They also collect information on chargebacks, and can flag up buyers that consistently lie in order to get free goods. Their database of the fraud-free transactions is just as important as the ones with issues. If a card is re-used at the same address and same IP address where it has previously been used with no problems, the transaction is probably safe.

298 DESIGN APPROPRIATE POLICIES.

Alongside these technical weapons the retailer needs to look at policies that can help prevent acceptance of fraudulent orders. With a policy-based approach, companies define what to do when fraud is suspected, which in turn may be flagged by technical indicators or orders over a certain value.

299 ACTION THESE POLICIES CONSISTENTLY.

Contacting the buyer by phone or email can be very effective, as fraudsters usually don't like to engage in dialogue – it's high risk for them. It may also become apparent that false details have been provided as a result of such contact. So you could call and say, "Hello Jerry, and your surname is?" Or ask the buyer for details of "the order". If the fraudster has placed multiple orders with multiple identities, they won't easily recall this information. Your suspicions should increase if questions take too long to answer. You could also request a fax of the credit card, bank statement, bill, driving licence or passport and this will most likely discourage a fraudster, although it may also irritate genuine customers. However, most will be happy to help once the reasons for your suspicion are explained.

300 GET ALTERNATIVE PAYMENT.

You can adopt another tactic if you are still suspicious of the order. Simply ask for payment by an alternative means, such as cheque. If a different card is offered, it would need to have the same billing address.

301 MAKE IT EASY FOR YOUR STAFF.

Your policies need to be crystal clear to all staff and full training must be given on how to explain the approach to customers so as not to alienate them.

302 ELIMINATE DELIVERY RISK WHERE POSSIBLE.

If possible use a delivery method that requires a signature, as this can help when the buyer denies they have received the goods. However, people may deliberately obscure their signatures and it isn't a guaranteed way to prove safe delivery. On the other hand, without a signature, you can't even begin to prove it.

303 GET THE BALANCE RIGHT.

It's difficult to find the right balance between over-zealous rejection of genuine business and losses from a lax approach. For instance, AVS will give up to 40% false negatives, due to the variety of address formats used by people, and AVS cannot be used on overseas orders. So AVS should only be used as one of several fraud indicators. Also, your business will turn out to have its own fraud profile, so using your own experience to develop specific policies is the best way to get this balance.

304 USE A PSP WITH THE RIGHT ANTI-FRAUD POLICIES.

The critical help that you need to implement all of these checks is the right payment service provider. So make sure that your payment provider supports 3D Secure, AVS, CV2, preferably one of the independent fraud checking services and is PCI DSS compliant. Once you have these services in operation, it's an idea to mention them on your web site to provide added reassurance to your customers.

The proportion of fraud is slightly decreasing despite the strong rise in web sales, so merchants are just winning the war against criminal activities. This is good news, but not grounds for complacency. Hopefully, with the right mix of tools and processes you can not only control fraud but also gain competitive advantage as you deal with it more effectively than the competition.

OPERATIONS

TIPS TO SHOW VISITORS THEIR TRANSACTIONS ARE SAFE

Once upon a time, customers needed convincing that the Internet was a safe place to shop. Internet novices still need that reassurance. But most people nowadays have shopped online at least once. They take it for granted that buying online is safe – but they still need to be persuaded that it's safe to buy from you. Here are some tips for convincing both groups.

Whether you deliver electronically or by carrier pigeon you face the same initial challenge. You need to establish trust. Customers cannot look around your premises to see how you store goods, how much dust is on them or whether your staff plays Frisbee with CDs. In a physical store, they can chat to the owner and look around. If they can see what they want on a shelf then they know it's in stock and in reasonable condition. You have to try to achieve the same confidence from your buyers.

305 REASSURE VISITORS THAT YOU ARE REAL.

As a vendor, you should list your actual address and phone number, and provide a point of contact where your web site visitors can speak to a real person. Say on the site: 'If you have any questions or queries about us or our products, please call us'. Provide facts about your business, and maybe pictures, as this will promote confidence. This point has been repeated from earlier. Deliberately. It's that important.

306 JOIN A PROFESSIONAL SCHEME

such as SafeBuy or the IMRG's Internet Shopping is Safe (ISIS) scheme. These provide reassurance for shoppers through a system of independent registration and verification of online retailers.

307 CREDIT CARD COMPANIES PROTECT BUYERS.

Many people don't realise the extent of protection that their credit card companies provide. It's simple. If you get transactions charged to your account which you didn't authorize, you can request a refund from your credit card issuer. So let them know.

308 BUYING ONLINE IS AS SAFE AS BUYING BY MAIL ORDER.

Risks on the Internet are the same as in mail order. If you feel confident to purchase by phone, fax or mail, you should be confident to buy on the Internet. In fact, your rights are the same whether shopping on the Net or in the high street. In the EU they are covered by the Distance Selling Directive; in the UK, by the Sale of Goods Act 1979 and the Trade Descriptions Act 1976 as well. If you receive faulty goods you have the right to a full refund. The only exception is when buying from abroad.

309 BUYING ONLINE IS NO RISKIER THAN MANY PERSONAL TRANSACTIONS.

The risk is actually no greater than using your card in a large store – where the person behind you can read it; or in a restaurant, where the card often disappears and could be skimmed and cloned.

310 USE A PSP.

Credit card information is fully encrypted by virtually all vendors as it travels over the net.

311 ALL OF THE BIG BOYS DO IT.

Billions of pounds of transactions are now being conducted across the Internet every month. This is despite viruses and all of the other problems. Thousands and thousands of purchases are taking place, and many huge companies such as Dell are making the web their main ordering mechanism. Would they do this if it was fundamentally insecure?

312 OFFER ALTERNATIVE ORDERING AND PAYMENT METHODS

As a vendor, even if you are pushing web sales hard you should give alternative ways of ordering such as by fax. A few people will take advantage of the facility, but for the rest it shows that you are fully confident. And offer additional methods of payment such as cheque and PayPal.

313 USE YOUR EXISTING CREDENTIALS.

If you are a member of a professional body, display their logo prominently on your home page – provided this is permitted under your terms of membership.

314 PRESENT CUSTOMER ENDORSEMENTS.

Whenever customers make positive comments about your company, try to get their permission to quote them on your web site. Scatter a few such endorsements around the site, and change them regularly.

315 PUT SOME PICTURES OF STAFF AND YOUR PREMISES IF YOU CAN.

It helps to establish how real you are, and is much more appealing than a faceless organisation. Take decent, sensible photos of your staff smiling, don't use their Facebook pictures!

OPERATIONS

15 TIPS TO BE LEGAL AND DECENT

Like every area of business these days, ecommerce is surrounded by a maze of red tape, rules and regulations. In fact, selling online tends to be worse because of the international dimension. And any slip-ups you make are there for the world to see – so it's doubly important to be legal and decent. These tips try to pull together some of the areas that you need to think about and understand. They shouldn't be taken as definitive – it's your responsibility to comply with the law – but they are a good place to start.

316 GET YOUR VAT REGISTRATION RIGHT.

You must be VAT registered if your annual sales exceed the current VAT threshold, which changes every year but is around £60,000 (Look on the Customs and Excise web site to get the most up-to-date figure). If you're not VAT registered, you don't have to worry about charging VAT and it would actually be against the law to do so.

317 UNDERSTAND TAX ON SHIPPING.

People often don't understand the finer points of VAT. For instance, if your products are a mixture of VATable and non-VATable, then the VAT charged on shipping should be in proportion to the mixture of VATable and non-VATable goods. Make sure your ecommerce solution can handle all of the VAT rules.

EXEMPT EU BUSINESS BUYERS FROM TAX.

If your customer is a non-UK business in the EU and is registered for VAT in their own country, they are allowed to quote their VAT registration number to you in order to be exempted from tax. If you can't accommodate this, those customers are likely to look elsewhere.

319 CHARGE THE COUNTRY VAT RATE IF YOU EXCEED THE COUNTRY VAT THRESHOLD.

Not many people know this, but if your online store is wildly successful and you are starting to turn over serious bucks selling into other EU countries, you hit some additional regulations. If you exceeded the individual VAT threshold for Germany, France, etc. then you should charge VAT at the appropriate VAT rate when selling into that country, not the usual UK 20% rate.

320 REMEMBER YOUR JURISDICTION.

We're in the EU so we are bound by EU rules. It's not the same when handling US buyers. US states might want to charge tax on sales into their area, but it's their responsibility to levy this tax. You don't have to charge this "use tax" which is between the buyer and the state where they live. So as a UK business you can sell into the US tax-free.

321 MAKE ORDERS AN "OFFER TO BUY".

Your terms and conditions should make orders from customers an "offer to buy". This way, if you have made a pricing mistake, are concerned about some aspect of the customer or have stock or delivery issues you can reject the order. Otherwise, if you took payment with the order you have contracted to supply the goods by default.

322 COMPLY WITH THE EU DISTANCE SELLING DIRECTIVE.

Under the EU Distance Selling Directive, you must make clear who you are by providing full contact details including an address and phone number. This is also good practice for building trust.

323 OFFER A 7-DAY RETURN OPTION.

Also under the EU Distance Selling Directive, you must accept goods for return within 7 working days. Provided you make this clear in your terms and conditions, your customers are responsible for the cost of returning the goods. However, you must refund the full cost of the products you sold along with the charge made for delivery. You are not entitled to charge a "restocking fee". There are a few exceptions to this right, for instance in the case of goods made-to-order, but the unconditional right applies to the vast majority of purchases made over the Internet or by telephone.

324 ALLOW FOR DISABLED VISITORS – IT'S THE LAW.

Make sure that you comply with the disability law, which came into effect in late 2004. The key requirement is that you have to take "reasonable" steps to provide access to people with disabilities, and this includes your online store. One way of doing that is to make sure that all images have alternate ('Alt') text tags so visually impaired people are still able to navigate your site.

325 PRIVACY MATTERS.

You probably need to register with the Data Protection Registry at www.dpr.gov.uk. Registering takes just a few hours of careful work and thought.

326 COMPLY WITH THE RULES ON SENDING EMAIL.

You are only allowed to send direct email marketing to individuals who have agreed to receive it from you by directly opting in. It is not sufficient simply to provide an opt-out. However, if you obtained their details in the course of making a sale the rules are different. You are allowed to continue communicating with them until they tell you otherwise, provided there is a free method of opting out each time you send them an email. You can use email for the opt-out.

327 IN CONCLUSION, TURN THESE RESPONSIBILITIES INTO BENEFITS.

Assuming that you are legal and decent, let the world know. Anything that adds to your credibility will help online. So why not list all of the things that you have done under the heading "We comply with the following legal and tax regulations"?

OPERATIONS

COMPLY WITH THE PAYMENT RULES

The vast majority of online transactions are paid for by credit or debit card. If your business has the right to take cards, known as "merchant status", then you must comply with various rules. Failure to comply can lead to increases in transaction charges, large fines or loss of merchant status. All of these can threaten the very survival of a web business. So here are ten tips for complying with the payment rules.

328 START WITH PAYPAL.

If you are a brand new start up, then it can be hard to achieve merchant status, which you need to accept card payments on your own behalf. So a great way is to accept credit and debit card payments through PayPal.

329 GET MERCHANT STATUS WHEN YOU CAN.

As soon as you are able to, get your own merchant status from the bank. It is normally considerably cheaper to have merchant status yourself than to take payments through PayPal.

330 BEWARE OF PCI DSS.

In an e-store, PCIDSS (which stands for Payment Card Industry Data Security Standard) is the single security standard for processing card payments and is supported by all banks, Visa, American Express and MasterCard. If your business accepts payment cards then it is compulsory to comply with PCIDSS, and you risk severe fines if you don't. You can familiarise yourself with the standard at https://www.pcisecuritystandards.org. The increase in online scams has prompted the card industry to start more rigorous enforcement of PCIDSS. This spells danger for small and medium sized online merchants. The problem with PCIDSS is that it takes a seventy-page document to describe it and although the regime for checking compliance is different based on the size of the merchant, the actual standard is the same.

331 LET A PSP HELP YOU WITH PCI COMPLIANCE.

For small businesses, the only feasible answer for proper compliance is to outsource the problem by letting a third party payment service provider (PSP) capture and store the card details. Perhaps surprisingly, this approach is relatively cheap and easy to implement, and a number of helpful services already exist, obviously including PayPal.

332 OBEY THE 3D SECURE RULES.

Visa and MasterCard have introduced a security standard for online payments called 3D Secure, which is also known as Verified by Visa and MasterCard SecureCode. This standard has now been made compulsory for some card types and usage is growing. You need to ensure that the payment technology that you supply is able to support 3D Secure.

333 OBEY THE CV2 RULES.

The CV2 (also known as CVC or "three digits on the strip on the back of your card") was introduced a few years ago to make phone and web payments more secure. The banks are trying to make the use of CV2 compulsory in all cases. It is also an iron rule that the CV2 cannot be stored on any computer system once the payment has been taken. Make sure that the payment solution that you adopt can obey these rules, as there are heavy fines for failing to comply.

334 IDENTIFY YOUR ECOMMERCE AND MOTO TRANSACTIONS PROPERLY.

Without getting too boring about further card rules, they state that you must clearly identify the type of card transaction – face to face, mail order or telephone (MOTO), or ecommerce. Payment service providers (PSPs) will do this for you. Keying ecommerce transactions into a PDQ terminal will break this rule.

335 RENEGOTIATE YOUR RATES REGULARLY.

Generally, the cheapest way of processing cards is to obtain merchant status. Unfortunately, the first time that you obtain an account the rates are generally very high. To compound this, even if your business grows substantially, no one will ever contact you from the bank to review your rates. The solution is to put a reminder in your diary to have a conversation with the bank. Before this, try to find out from a few other businesses what they are paying. Things will go much better if they are along the lines of "my friend in the same business pays x%, while I'm paying y%. Please match this rate or I will be forced to move." One company that we were advising made a sixty thousand pound saving per annum from a single phone call.

336 SPLATTER YOU SITE WITH PAYMENT LOGOS.

If you take the cards, why not show them on your site? It looks professional and adds credibility. Of course, you should follow any restrictions placed on the display of logos, or at least do so if they are pointed out to you.

337 INTEGRATE PAYMENTS WITH OPERATIONS.

It is important that your ecommerce software is designed to work seamlessly in co-operation with whatever payment gateway (PSP) that you choose. The key is a tight integration that will allow your software to instruct the PSP to make charges against the card, refund payments and so on. Not only does this integration make the merchant's life considerably easier, it also guarantees a safe transaction as the card can only be transacted against the individual merchant against whom the cardholder made an original payment.

MARKET PLACES

MARKET PLACES

EBAY, AMAZON AND FACEBOOK

The last few years have seen the rise of market places eBay and Amazon as well as others such as Play.com. There are tremendous benefits with market places but there are some downsides too.

The downside of market places is why in this publication we mostly consider running your own store, but you may find that a market place is a useful adjunct to this. As a result, here are some tips to provide a broad background in the use of market places. We shall also touch on selling on Facebook.

338 DON'T MISS THE EBAY OR AMAZON BOAT.

The web is big business, and the top dogs include eBay and Amazon. Getting in their slipstream as they grow ever more powerful must be considered.

339 UNDERSTAND THE SIZE OF THE EBAY OPPORTUNITY.

Forbes magazine states that eBay has around 100 million current users in the world. There are around 200 million products listed at any one time and over 10 million of these are added or delisted each day. eBay themselves say that around 100,000 buyers join them each day. The UK boasts to the order of 16 million eBay visitors per month, so it has a major share of total sales and some entrepreneurs have achieved fantastic results. eBay recently stated that five businesses had made more than £1m sales in their first year, and they expect a tenth of businesses to eventually achieve sales of over £3m.

340 UNDERSTAND THE SIZE OF THE AMAZON OPPORTUNITY.

Around 30% of sales on the Amazon platform are third-party sales (i.e. made by merchants other than Amazon). The percentage is roughly static and so third party merchant sales are growing at the same outstanding rate (around 40%) as total Amazon sales. It should however be noted that the number of people selling on Amazon has also grown substantially, so the average merchant has not seen the same growth as the platform. When you compare Amazon with Walmart, the world's largest retailer, you see how phenomenal their business performance is. Amazon has grown much more rapidly in its first fifteen years than Walmart did in its formative stage. So there's an argument to get onside with Amazon while there is still time.

341 THINK LIKE A FRANCHISEE.

Selling on Amazon or eBay is like taking on a franchise. They provide a lot of support, but you have to play by the franchise rules, with the franchiser taking a big share of the spoils. These market places can let you both build and expand your businesses, but make sure you own the long term value. The tips here try to enable you to take advantage of the opportunities while minimising the risks.

342 PROMOTE YOUR OWN STORE.

It may be a good idea to think of the marketplaces a little like advertising, you are promoting your products and service for a price, generally the listing or commission fee. Maximise the opportunity by including a flyer or marketing brochure for your own store, possibly with a discount for coming direct.

343 UNDERSTAND THE BENEFITS OF MARKETPLACES.

Market places enable you to start getting visitors straight away and hence to start selling quickly. This is a huge benefit and is the reason why large numbers of merchants have started their selling online through this route. Many merchants with their own web sites also sell through Amazon, eBay and others. Many new start-ups are initially weak in marketing and that's where the market places really help. Tens of millions of buyers search them every month, so if you have the right products at the right price with great service, you will make sales. Other reasons for using market places include the following: low start up costs because no money needs to be spent on marketing or technology; you are effectively addressing a captive market of people already searching on the market places; payment options have already been sorted out; you can choose between auctioning products and fixed price sales (eBay only); extra services are provided such as leaflets that can be dispatched with orders plus emails promoting repeat business (eBay only) and provision on business loans for expansion (Amazon only); fraud protection; community of other merchants who can help; provision of warehousing, picking and delivery service (Amazon only). If you already sell on your own ecommerce site, then it's worth thinking about adding eBay and Amazon. They won't work for everyone, but the opportunity shouldn't be ignored.

344 UNDERSTAND THE ISSUES WITH MARKETPLACES.

The benefits are straightforward, so it's worth outlining the problems. First there is the cost. The transaction and listing fees are expensive. The second issue is control. You must obey the strict rules of the marketplaces or your business can be suspended in an instant. The last disadvantage would be comical, if it wasn't so real. It's not hard to find stories of merchants who have been cut off in their prime if you search online. That's why we strongly advise businesses to never solely rely on one market place.

345 KEEP THE RISK UNDER CONTROL.

It is certainly possible to build a business just on market places, and it can be an excellent strategy to get started. But the downside risk is real, so it's important to grow into other channels such as your own stand-alone ecommerce store as you become successful. The reasons to go beyond market places are: to find channels where higher margins can be sustained by avoiding the fees and unrelenting pricing pressure; to reduce the risk; and to expand sales. You need to always be looking for changes to get to a more successful formula and to minimise risk. Harvard Business Review studied successful entrepreneurs a few years ago and found that they weren't blind risk takers. One of the common factors among the most successful was a good ability to assess risk. The danger with market places is that you build their business more than your own.

346 UNDERSTAND THE MARKET PLACE PRICING DYNAMIC.

Due to the competition, prices on market places are generally lower than on alternative channels, although a few merchants can manage to achieve higher prices to offset the fees. The fact that it is so easy to start up on eBay and Amazon is a double-edged sword. eBay and Amazon help to level the playing field with the big boys, which is good. Against this is that they encourage swathes of new, naive sellers. A lot of these are new to business and think they should compete by having low prices. They don't last long as they lose money for a while and then drop out. Unfortunately, they are then replaced by more of the same. In the meantime they devastate everyone's margins.

347 GET YOUR PRICING RIGHT.

To get your pricing right you first need to fully understand your own costs, including all aspects like labour, returns, charge-backs, breakages, packing materials, delivery and market place fees. You cannot scrimp, as poor feedback will destroy your business. Look at the same or similar products to your own and track the high and low prices over time.

Keep this in a spreadsheet or database so you have a quick reference when setting your prices. Remember that "loss leaders" are simply likely to be loss makers when most people are looking for only one item. The only excuse to sell at low prices is to do so for a limited period in order to build up substantial positive feedback prior to moving to realistic prices. One merchant comments: "We know that Amazon's proposition is attractive to certain buyers, even though our products are slightly more expensive on Amazon compared to our own site, we still get about 10% of sales via Amazon. So Amazon is a useful channel - what I think we are realising is that it is also a 'High Risk' channel so we price accordingly". This comes from their experience of Amazon adjudicating in favour of buyers on most customer disputes. It's best to either have a unique product or price somewhat above the lowest. Chasing prices to the bottom will never result in business success.

348 PROVIDE GREAT SERVICE.

Great service on market places is the single most critical factor. It means and packing items well, dispatching them promptly and using good couriers to ensure they arrive on time and in great condition.

The principle applied by the market places is that the customer is always right. Customers rate you and even when you are almost perfect, a few misguided individuals will still give you poor ratings. If you get many low ratings you will get almost no orders, and below a certain threshold you will be thrown off the platform. Yes really. So respond as quickly as you can to incoming orders and never be found selling items that are out of stock.

Good packing materials are a must as nothing destroys more value than the delivery of damaged goods where everyone loses. One merchant with 100% positive feedback and a degree of hyperbole advised me: "Find packing materials that can withstand a nuclear explosion, it's hard to keep 100% positive feedback". Your quality of carrier is critical both for speed, certainty and quality. You will find some carriers sometimes claim to have left a card at a customer's premises but haven't even been there, others toss things into gardens as a form of delivery when they are in a hurry.

The appearance of the driver and van, the persistence in trying to get the door answered, and their collection of a proof of delivery or leaving a card all make a massive impression. So watch them like a hawk. Offering a no questions refund for a reasonable time is well worth the cost as it minimises time and morale-sapping disputes and negative feedback.

Good service is impossible to over-emphasise. Unfortunately it's all about huge attention to detail and hard work.

349 CONSIDER EXPORTING USING EBAY AND AMAZON.

It's easier to start selling overseas on a market place than from your own store as you don't need to market in the overseas territory, generally the market places will be much more trusted than a site found overseas on Google and a lot of the needed infrastructure is already in place. Just remember that the cost of shipping is usually much greater. You must allow for some non-payers and potential fraud risk too. Some of the most successful eBay based businesses have developed exports as a very major part of their business. eBay state that 98% of business turning over more than one million pounds boosted takings through overseas sales. The top export markets for UK retailers are the United States, Ireland, France, Australia and Germany.

MARKET PLACES

SELL ON EBAY

A friend of mine has run a successful business on eBay since the year 2000, with both a shop and an auction. He provided many interesting thoughts and these have been weaved into the tips below.

350 UNDERSTAND THE FIRST EBAY KEY TO SUCCESS.

As discussed in the previous section, the first key to success when selling on eBay is great service. Without this, you will see few orders and maybe be banned from the platform. That's why you need to be clear on your pricing. You can choose to either sell at a loss with brilliant service while you build your positive feedback, or price from the start at a level which enables you to provide great service. Giving poor service because you have to sell cheaply to get started will result in immediate failure. This point has been repeated – it's that important.

351 DECIDE ON AN AUCTION OR BUY IT NOW.

You can sell two ways on eBay. The original eBay auction is exactly what you expect. You set a reserve price, a time for the auction and the person with the highest bid at the end wins, provided the reserve is beaten. The second method means you sell like a traditional shop with fixed prices for each product, this is called Buy It Now. The latter is most like other forms of ecommerce and Amazon. Auction is probably most appropriate for collectable items, things that are rare and second hand items where it's harder to price them.

352 UNDERSTAND EBAY AUCTION PRICING.

Auctions are unpredictable and the phrase "you win some, you lose some" is a perfect description of the dilemma. You must keep your nerve and avoid over-cooking the minimum price. Taking a risk with a low starting price will really attract attention, and is less risky for popular items. That's why you should sell in an area where you have some knowledge.

The single most important thing is to have done your homework on the competition by looking hard at numerous previous auctions. See the bidding patterns and learn from this to make your own plans. If you really can't afford any risk then set the minimum price close to your cost.

353 FIND YOUR BEST STRATEGY.

On the one hand, eBay is the number one web site in the world for collectibles. On the other, eBay presents a daunting challenge as a lot of competition is on price. If you do not already have a high volume business, it's hard to compete successfully. You can tackle this problem in two ways. The first is to try to find a niche within a niche. Here, you define your specialist area down to the point where you can provide the most expertise, the greatest experience in sourcing parts plus the widest product range. With time you can expand from this beachhead into related areas. An example might be boat spares. If the general category is too competitive, and so is "motor boat spares", you could just do Fairline spares (one particular make of motor-cruiser) initially. The second way is to utilise the fact that in general the more expensive the product the bigger the margin. The cause is partly because start-ups avoid more expensive items presumably due to the cost of stock. The result is that competition is less fierce. Of course, mistakes in purchasing expensive items, breakages, fraud and returns will be costly and painful. You take more risk, more care is required but the rewards are greater.

354 STATE YOUR CONDITIONS CLEARLY.

Try to be as clear as possible on your conditions of sale. Understand that not everyone will read them, so if you have anything unusual it will lead to negative feedback. You should cover delivery options, payments methods and your returns policy. These all need consideration in the light of your margins.

355 UNDERSTAND THE EBAY COSTS.

eBay charges an "insertion fee" every time an item is listed which can range from zero to £1.30. They also take the selling price and charge a percentage of typically 10% up to a maximum of £40. Paypal will charge an additional percentage of typically 3%.

356 RESEARCH EBAY FULLY.

Knowledge is power and the eBay community forums are full of information and advice. It is well worth spending time there, see http://community.ebay.co.uk.

MARKET PLACES

SELL ON AMAZON

As described earlier, Amazon has seen amazing growth but they are also known for their draconian policies. The tips here have been drawn up by talking to real Amazon sellers with real life stories of their experiences.

357 UNDERSTAND AMAZON.

Amazon particularly ensures that is easy for buyers to compare the same products and therefore to buy just on price and service (see tip on EAN below). This is probably part of their heritage of selling books and CDs. Michael Jackson's Bad is the same whoever you buy it from. It may be good for Amazon, but margins are squeezed to the bone for merchants.

358 UNDERSTAND THE FIRST AMAZON KEY TO SUCCESS.

To steal a common cliché, there are four keys to success on Amazon. These are good service, good service, good service and good service. Your pricing must provide enough margin for this good service. Like with eBay, you need to either be prepared to endure a loss in the formative stages of your business while your rating is built up, or you need to charge enough that enables you to provide such service while making a profit. Poor service will guarantee failure on Amazon more than anything else. This point has been repeated yet again – it really is that important.

59 UNDERSTAND THE AMAZON USE OF EAN.

Amazon ensures that the same products can be compared by insisting that everything for sale on their platform has an EAN bar code, which they then map to an ASIN (Amazon Single Identification Number). Existing products should already have this code and your manufacturer or distributor can provide it. If your manufacture or exclusively source the item yourself, you must get an approved bar code, which is expensive. The big advantage is that once you have acquired the bar code, then as the owner you can limit competition.

360 GET APPROVED BY AMAZON.

First, Amazon must approve you to sell, which normally means you are a limited company with an existing trading history. Some categories are open e.g. books, and anyone can sell within them. Others are closed and Amazon must give you explicit approval.

361 UNDERSTAND THE LISTING PROCESS.

If you want to sell an item on Amazon, you first provide the bar code. If this is already present in the Amazon database the images and description will be automatically used and this means that products can be put up for sale very quickly and easily. That's why selling on Amazon is about price and service – there aren't really any other differentiators. This database is actually built by Amazon merchants and you can add missing products yourself once you have achieved trusted status.

362 UNDERSTAND THE AMAZON SALES PROCESS.

When a prospect looks for something on Amazon, Amazon will display all of the merchants that can supply that item. The first (if applicable) will always be Amazon themselves, then third party merchants will appear ranked by service and price, together with the available stock level. You decide which international markets that you sell to so you will dictate whether your results appear when people search from other countries.

363 UNDERSTAND THE ORDERING AND PAYMENT PROCESS.

Orders placed by buyers of your products will appear in SellerCentral (Amazon's portal for their merchants) under your account. You must fulfil those orders in the time you stated and Amazon then carefully tracks this. Amazon pays merchants every two weeks after the deduction of their fees.

364 UNDERSTAND FULFILLMENT BY AMAZON.

For a price, Amazon will store and deliver your products. Merchants log into their account to say what they are sending to Amazon and then send the actual items. Amazon charge for storage (with a higher Christmas charge). When you use this feature, you appear higher in Amazon's list when buyers search and bad feedback is automatically deleted! As a result, it might be a good option to get started.

365 UNDERSTAND THE AMAZON RESTRICTIONS.

As far as Amazon is concerned, they own the customer; merchants only get the customer's physical address, not email, telephone number or any other details. Some merchants place their company's sticker on all deliveries to try to establish a stronger link with customers.

366 UNDERSTAND YOU ARE COMPETING WITH AMAZON.

Amazon has a nasty habit. They can see the sales statistics across their entire site, including all third party sales. This means that they can see what is selling well and that includes products that they don't themselves stock. I know of several cases where merchants have had a particularly successful and unique sales line, only to find themselves shortly afterwards competing directly with Amazon. One was actually called by Amazon and asked where they got their stock. Shortly afterwards, Amazon was competing on that product and surprise, surprise, sales had dropped. This is a great business for Amazon. Other people scour the world for interesting new products and take all of the risk to see if it works. If it does, Amazon opens up shop and takes a lot of the profit.

367 DO NOT WHOLLY DEPEND ON AMAZON.

Apart from the fact that you can be banned from their platform with no recourse, you are competing with them so don't leave your whole business reliant on them.

368 UNDERSTAND AMAZON COSTS.

Amazon charges a minimum fee of £25 a month and then a variable fee per item sold which varies from 10 – 20% of the sale price depending on the product category and is non-negotiable. It's not cheap.

369 UNDERSTAND AMAZON SERVICE FEEDBACK.

Every time a purchase is made on Amazon the buyer is asked if they wish to give feedback. The feedback is given on a star rating system and has a dramatic impact on sales. Service is rated on: cancellation rate where the target is less than 2.5% of orders are cancelled before dispatch; the order defect rate which consists of an "A-Z guarantee claim", or a card chargeback or negative feedback and the target is less than 1% orders assessed as defective; delayed dispatch rate based on information supplied by the merchant where the target is 5% or less. Each of the above has a rating of good, fair or poor. The merchant needs green ticks for all categories else they are assessed as having violated policy and will get a warning call from Amazon. They then usually have a few weeks to improve or be kicked off the market place.

370 RESEARCH AMAZON FULLY.

Again, knowledge is power and the Amazon community forums, like eBay are crammed with helpful information. Time spent is a good investment, see the Amazon seller forums at http://www.amazonsellercommunity.com/forums/.

MARKET PLACES

SELL ON FACEBOOK

A lot of fuss has been made about ecommerce on Facebook, but the truth is that hardly any physical goods are being sold directly from Facebook. However, Facebook is a power to be reckoned with and there are opportunities, so here is a consideration of this channel.

371 DON'T SELL UNTIL YOU'RE SOCIAL.

Before you consider a Facebook store, integrate social networking into your main store. There are whole sections on using Facebook and Twitter for this purpose elsewhere in these tips.

372 KNOW HOW TO SETUP A STORE ON FACEBOOK.

You can now sell directly from Facebook and this is an option worth considering (but see below too). You achieve this by adding a storefront tab to your official page. Some small businesses are starting to use this as a cheap way to add an independent, secondary, web store. To start, you need a store platform. There are many suppliers with similar features and similar prices. A lot of noise comes from specialist Facebook marketing companies, but then they would be keen, wouldn't they?

373 DON'T RELY TOTALLY ON FACEBOOK.

It is reported that Facebook stores typically generate less than 1% of total ecommerce revenue for retailers that already have successful web businesses, as reported by Forester Research. So with very low traditional ecommerce sales, the vast majority of the billions of dollars per annum spent on Facebook is related to games and advertising. Where games use Facebook credits, Facebook take a 30% margin. It appears that the most successful products on Facebook have viral aspects. This is where recommendation by friends is most important so it's not unexpected that the most successful Facebook stores sell books, movies and entertainment.

374 USE FACEBOOK STORES AS AN ADD ON.

It really only makes sense to use Facebook as a complementary channel to the rest of your ecommerce business. This keeps risk down and attempts to capture revenue that would otherwise be missed, while maintaining a presence on Facebook, where ecommerce may yet take off. New initiatives are continuously being announced, so stay in touch.

375 KEEP WORK TO A MINIMUM.

You need to make sure that it is easy to maintain your Facebook store. The volume of sales probably won't justify a lot of work at this early stage.

TOP TIPS **376–414**

ADVANCED ECOMMERCE

ADVANCED ECOMMERCE

SELL ABROAD

Successful business owners are always looking for new ways to expand sales, and those running web stores are no exception. Most would like to make overseas sales, but this can seem like a scary prospect. With the Internet being a global medium, any web store potentially has access to a worldwide market. This potential represents an opportunity, so here we'll look at some of the challenges presented by international sales, including the areas of tax, shipping and fraud. So here are top tips for selling overseas.

376 FLAUNT BEING BRITISH.

Firstly, and surprising as it is to some of us who live here, the UK still has an excellent reputation around the world. So if we've got it we should flaunt it – make it clear to buyers that you're based here.

377 REALISE WHAT AN ADVANTAGE BEING ENGLISH SPEAKERS IS.

The second inbuilt advantage is speaking English. It is the first language of many countries, not least the US. Therefore, you can make a lot of progress without translating your web site, although the best long term results would obviously require translation into major languages.

378 DON'T TAKE THINGS FOR GRANTED.

While there is opportunity, it's important not to assume that just because you have succeeded in the UK you will succeed elsewhere. Every market is different and has its special quirks. You may fail abroad for a combination of reasons varying from better, more entrenched or deeper pocketed competitors to a different culture, statutory environment, or maybe stage of market development. Any of these can apply, even when you are selling what is fundamentally the same type of product to the same kind of customer.

379 GIVE IT A TRY.

However, the web provides the ability to insert a toe in the water for international sales, and come up with an initial assessment of how competitive you are. Organising a small scale trial makes a lot of sense and can be done at hugely lower cost and lower risk than would have been required prior to the advent of the web.

380 MONETISE YOUR EXPERTISE INTERNATIONALLY.

The Internet was designed as a global communications medium, and its impact in the area of international trade is growing all the time. The good news is that much of the expertise that you use to get UK visitors to check out your site can be re-used for the international market. In particular, skills in search engine optimisation (SEO) and pay-per-click advertising (PPC) can also be applied to attract visitors from abroad. Yet all of this can be organised from the comfort of your own office. It really is different from the past, and overseas marketing has become an order of magnitude easier.

381 GET THE TAX RIGHT.

If your customer is a non-UK business in the EU and is registered for VAT in their own country, they are allowed to quote their VAT registration number to you in order to be exempted from tax. If you can't accommodate this, those customers are likely to look elsewhere. New regulations on how this works came in 1 January 2010, so it's worth confirming the details with

HMRC www.hmrc.gov.uk/vat/managing/international/overseas-traders.html. It's not the same when handling US buyers. US states might want to charge tax on sales into their area, but it's their responsibility to levy this tax. You don't have to charge this "use tax" which is between the buyer and the state where they live. As a UK business you can sell into the US tax free – but you should make your customers aware that they could be charged tax on the goods when they are imported.

382 LEARN HOW TO TAKE OVERSEAS PAYMENTS.

If you're eating out in France and you pay by card then the restaurant will be paid in Euros. Your card company will automatically translate the amount into pounds and that is what will appear on your statement, with the original currency and amount noted alongside. Buying across the net is exactly the same - there's no absolute need for a multi-currency system in your web store. However, one handy tool is a conversion facility that can provide an indicative amount in the potential buyer's local currency. An alternative is to run a full multi-currency store, or even have separate sites for each country and currency. You don't need to support every obscure currency; sites in US dollars and Euros will cover a big part of the market. Taking this approach does however expose you to currency risk, although supporting multiple currencies will be best if you are really serious about your overseas business.

383 WATCH OUT FOR FRAUD.

Possibly the biggest problem to consider when selling abroad is fraud. Orders from abroad are more likely to be from scamsters simply because it's easier for them to get away with it. Generally the police are not interested in small-scale fraud, and even less so when the crime is committed outside their jurisdiction. In addition, many of the fraud prevention systems such as address checking don't work with most overseas cards. There are several ways that fraudsters work. If the person was using stolen credit card details, the amount is likely to be charged back to you once the true owner becomes aware of the charge. Even someone who genuinely ordered and received the goods can dispute payment. There's a whole section on fraud elsewhere. Depending on your products, it is just possible that fraud will be such a problem with overseas orders that you can't accept them. If you are worried about a particular order, it may be worth insisting on an electronic payment (not payment card) before you ship.

384 GET THE SHIPPING RIGHT.

Nowadays, shipping abroad is pretty straight forward, although it's very likely that the best international carrier will be different from your regular carrier. You can make it easier by using a recognised international carrier such as UPS, Fedex or DHL, who can advise you of any issues.

385 GET CUSTOMS DECLARATIONS RIGHT.

Completing a customs declaration is a must, but as long as what you are sending is legal in the country that you're selling it to, this should not pose a problem. Most of the retail world leaves customs or import duties to the purchaser. They are responsible for any of these charges, so you can ignore them. However, you must say explicitly in your terms and conditions that any charges are down to the buyer. However, you must have the correct customs declaration on your goods but your shipper should be able to help. If your sales grow you will learn more about this whole area and be in a better position to advise your buyer. There are different procedures for trade sales, so you would need to investigate these if you are operating in this field.

386 THINK DIFFERENTLY INTERNATIONALLY.

Although the emphasis up until now has been on how relatively easy it is to sell overseas, there are differences, and once you begin to see some success, focusing on these differences will grow sales further. The next few tips cover the main points.

387 LOOK AT LOCAL SEARCH LEADERS.

There are many search engines specific to countries, as a visit to www.searchenginecolossus.com will show. So, it is important for international brands to achieve visibility in local market search engines. Local search engines with significant market share include Baidu in China, Voila in France and Yandex in Russia and Miva in the US. These are worth investigating.

388 TRANSLATE INTO MULTIPLE LANGUAGES.

Although English is very commonly spoken, not everyone speaks it and everyone is more comfortable when text is translated into his or her native language. For this reason, local translation is a must if your international business is to become really significant.

389 REMEMBER CULTURAL DIFFERENCES.

Your translation needs to be done by a native to avoid the comical mistakes that invariable arise when a non-native does a translation. Remember that the way things are presented will vary from one culture to another. For instance, US advertising is much more direct (almost embarrassingly so to our eyes) than UK advertising.

390 SELL IN THE LOCAL CURRENCY.

If you really want to succeed on a big scale, you must eventually start selling in the currency that the locals most commonly use.

391 CONSIDER TIME DIFFERENCES.

Local time differences will impact any strategy around time of day for search engine marketing, the same for emails and access to telephone lines. On this point, it is possible to provide a local number that comes through to the UK, but it must be manned for their time zone! Use Google Analytics to show you exactly how many visitors your site is receiving from abroad and at what time of day this occurs.

ADVANCED ECOMMERCE

BE MOBILE READY

If you're anything like the typical e-commerce merchant I talk to, you're probably obsessed with site statistics. Within the space of a few years Google analytics has turned rational thinking retailers into stats-a-holics.

I recently spent a day with a merchant who could tell me everything about his customers, where they lived, the browser and ISP they use and most importantly the paths customers take through the site. However, the one fact he couldn't tell me was how many people visited his site from an Apple iPhone.

Come to think of it he wasn't sure if iPhone users could even use his site. With the rapid growth of smart phones the mobile web is truly with us. So in these tips we explore just how ecommerce and mobile are converging.

392 STAY ON TOP OF MOBILE TRENDS.

The mobile arena is currently both the fastest changing technology sector and the fastest changing ecommerce sector. So monitor what is going on and make sure that you ecommerce site can work with both the most popular mobiles used for browsing the web, but also those that are growing fast.

393 CATCH ANY MOBILE PAYMENT TREND.

It looks like mobiles are becoming the new device for making payments so stay on top of this trend too.

394 MAKE THE RIGHT CALL FOR YOUR DEMOGRAPHICS.

Depending on who you are targeting, mobile may be more or less important. So ask the question, how many of MY customers want to buy using their mobile? Who are you trying to reach? Where and how are they visiting your web site? What does the typical visitor do at your site?

395 HAVE A SMART PHONE THEME.

The fact that many smart phones can browse the main web can be misleading. Even though it's true, most sites with their wide screens and nice pictures aren't suitable for mobiles due to screen size and slow connections. So consider having a theme which provides a much more compact version of your store optimised for mobiles. However, remember that customers often want to see large images and have the convenience of a keyboard so actual traditional ecommerce buying is smaller on mobile than general usage might indicate.

396 UNDERSTAND PATTERNS OF USE.

Discovering the "where and how" of mobile use is a hard. People use mobile devices in so many different ways and in so many different places. The long standing mantra has always been to make your site usable under the worst conditions possible. Now this may not sound particularly appealing but your mobile site needs to work on both fast Wi-Fi and the slower 3G signal. It's the same with screen estate and input devices, catering for both large touch screens as well as smaller devices that may require a stylus or keyboard. Understanding how your customers will use your mobile site is also critical. Are they using their mobiles to purchase goods, check prices or simply looking for store information such as an address? Gaining this customer insight will define the very essence of your mobile site.

397 MAKE YOUR PLANS.

Mobile commerce is on a tear, and understanding who, what and how needn't be all that difficult. My advice is simple, do your research. Think like your customers. Put together an action plan.

ADVANCED ECOMMERCE

SELL THROUGH MULTIPLE CHANNELS

Multi-channel retailing is one of the current areas of excitement in retail, and there is strong statistical evidence for the view that shoppers who use multiple channels actually spend at a higher level than average. By multi-channel retailing we mean selling through high street stores, online stores, telephone, market places like eBay and other routes such as unattended kiosks. In our company, we identified this as a potential high growth area some years ago, however its value is only just becoming apparent. The following merely scratch the surface of the points to be considered when implementing a multi-channel strategy. So here are some tips for making a success of your multi-channel business.

There are many cultural challenges to introducing multi-channel to a business. Management may take the view that a particular channel is not mainstream for the business. It is however interesting to note that the previous views that the Internet didn't apply to a particular sectors e.g. insurance and fashion have long since been proved widely off the mark. However, major challenges remain where senior management are unfamiliar with particular channels, business is in a state of flux so doesn't want to make a major commitment in new areas, specialist skills are required which the company doesn't possess, unknown levels of investment are required, and technology and buyers behaviour is changing rapidly. A rational case must always be built by examining evidence of customer benefits, growth in particular channels and also what the competitors are doing.

398 LEARN FROM THE BIG GUYS.

More than 80% of the top retailers in the UK already sell online, but for well established but small retailers the figure is still well under 50%. It is interesting to note that most national retailers have seen their online store become their "biggest store" in an 18-30 month timeframe from start-up. The keys that they found for multi-channel success was to set up a multi-function team to implement the strategy; to get external input; to give a lot of focus and attention in the early days; to experiment and learn; to communicate well both internally and externally; to integrate the operations correctly to provide web based facilities for customer service people so that they can see everything the customer can see; and to allocate costs and benefits to local stores based on postcode so that they fully co-operate with returns and people who browse in store and state that they want to buy online.

399 THINK ABOUT THE HUMANS.

One reason Tesco have been successful online is that regional and store managers are rewarded for web sales in their area. Cultural issues are critical in getting a multi-channel strategy to work, especially in large organisations.

400 CONSOLIDATE YOUR SALES DATA.

One of the biggest challenges of multi-channel is data. The need to consolidate into single view and also the need to extend KPIs to each channel. According to Gartner, order, inventory and product data must be disseminated across channels to produce a channel-agnostic customer experience.

401 BE HONEST.

Be completely honest about pricing. A company was recently caught with two web sites. One had the same as in-store prices and was used by store staff to demonstrate their prices were the same in-store as on the web. The other was the real online store and had lower prices.

402 UNDERSTAND BEHAVIOUR.

To understand customer experience at the web site, you need to look at web analytics but also observer people interacting with the company (web site, call centre etc) under lab conditions and ask them how they are feeling about things as they go through.

403 TREAT THE WEB AS ANOTHER STORE.

Do this from a stock, reporting, investment and business performance point of view. The web is just another way of making money; it should neither be favoured nor discriminated against. The current greater growth rate in web sales should, however, be taken into account as this is a business factor.

404 CONSIDER HOW CHANNELS CAN HELP EACH OTHER.

In a Royal Mail survey of nearly a thousand UK consumers, nearly half had looked through a catalogue before buying online, 44% of those who didn't shop from home had browsed a catalogue before buying in-store, 22% had browsed online before making an in-store purchase. Shoppers who had browsed a catalogue prior to making a web purchase spent 25% more than other online shoppers. It's well worth considering this in your plans.

405 PUSH BUYING ACROSS CHANNELS.

Offers to customers should be dependent on their characteristics and can be used very effectively to drive people across channels e.g. offer double points for the web purchase of a gift voucher of more than £20 to a price sensitive customer, and offer a complementary makeover at cosmetics counter when a good customer purchases a gift voucher more than £20. Retailers that have tried this have seen a measurable improvement in profit.

406 MAXIMISE YOUR PROFIT.

Do pricing and offers by channel to maximise profit. One company was quoted as having costs per order of 12-15p on the web, £4-5 catalogue/call centre and £10-15 in store. Digital acquisition cost is also much lower.

407 EXPLOIT MULTIPLE CHANNELS TO MAXIMUM EFFECT.

There can be unexpected benefits from multi-channel selling, such as the ability to clear surplus or end of line stock through alternative channels and also to benefit from the long tail effect. This is where people want to buy something but it isn't economical for a store to stock or display it. By providing an in store terminal or kiosk, such items can be viewed and ordered, thus profitably supplying the need.

408 SUPPORT ALL CHANNELS.

Organise yourself to properly support any new channel, for instance answer emails in a timely way.

409 REMEMBER THE CUSTOMER.

The heart of multi-channel is allowing the customer to interact with you in the way they choose. The systems, processes and staff training to provide multi-channel should be assembled while always thinking about your customer. The customer must be the centre of your multi-channel solutions.

410 KEEP PRICES THE SAME IN DIFFERENT CHANNELS.

Having headline prices the same across all channels will avoid debates with customers. You can still differentiate pricing through shipping charges or special discounts only available in one channel.

411 PROVIDE A CONSISTENT PRODUCT RANGE.

As far as possible, have the same range available online and in store. That way, people who research in one channel and then try to buy in another won't be disappointed.

412 CAPTURE EVERY POSSIBLE ORDER.

If it's out of stock, make sure it can be ordered for home delivery, from another store, or online.

413 AVOID DAMAGING YOUR BRAND.

Common sense tells us that consumers see a single brand whether they are looking at a web store or the related retail outlets. So make sure the experience is equally good in every channel.

414 INTEGRATE YOUR BACK OFFICE APPROPRIATELY.

Integration of systems can be expensive, unless your whole operation is based on a package that already provides integration. So do your research.

TOP TIPS **415–438**

CUSTOMER RELATIONS, REPEAT BUSINESS AND RECOMMENDATIONS

CUSTOMER RELATIONS, REPEAT BUSINESS AND RECOMMENDATIONS

WAYS TO SHOW CUSTOMERS YOU CARE

It's one thing to present a great appearance to a new customer and win their first order. Now you have to deliver the service you have led them to expect! If you can demonstrate that you really look after your customers and give them a great experience, they are very likely to come back and order again and again. The simple key to showing customers you care is to ask what you would like if you were a customer.

415 DON'T TALK ABOUT IT, DO IT.

If there's anything worse than bad service, it's receiving bad service after you've been told how great the service is. It's much better to actually provide good service than deliver platitudes about it.

416 ONCE THEY HAVE PLACED AN ORDER WITH YOU, SEND AN IMMEDIATE ACKNOWLEDGEMENT THAT YOU HAVE RECEIVED IT.

This can be automated by your ecommerce package or you may choose to send a personal note. It is much easier for small companies to offer such personal touches than for corporates with their larger volume of orders.

417 KEEP THE CUSTOMER INFORMED.

If you can afford it, pro-actively monitor deliveries. Find out from your carriers what didn't get delivered as promised, then contact your customer to let them know what's happening. Customers will think this is great service, and it turns a failure into a demonstration that you care.

418 GO MULTI CHANNEL.

If you have a printed catalogue, ask if they would like a copy when they order. Don't feel that the web is your only channel – you have multiple routes to your customer. It is much easier and cheaper to sell more to an existing customer than it is to win a new one. Research suggests that customers who buy through multiple channels are the most profitable customers.

419 LOOK FOR EVERY OPPORTUNITY TO PERSONALISE YOUR SERVICE.

The Internet is generally very impersonal, so you need to communicate that your business is run by human beings who care about their customers. This also reassures them that they have a contact, if there is any problem – it is much better than a faceless corporation.

420 IMAGE IS AN ISSUE WHEN A CUSTOMER HAS NEVER MET YOU.

Take all the chances you have to exceed expectations and build your reputation. If you need to call a customer for any reason – for example for security purposes, if the credit card and delivery addresses are different – take the opportunity to offer something extra such as a gift-wrap service. This helps protect you without offending the customer.

421 IF THERE ARE ANY PROBLEMS, LIKE OUT OF STOCK ITEMS OR A PROBLEM WITH DELIVERY, TELL THE CUSTOMER IMMEDIATELY AND TAKE FULL RESPONSIBILITY.

Never, ever blame anyone else – even the courier. Nothing is more infuriating for the consumer than when a supplier blames some third-party over whom they have no control.

422 WHEN A MISTAKE HAPPENS, CORRECT IT AT THE HIGHEST LEVEL.

Customers appreciate it when a manager calls, rather than the most junior person – it makes them feel important to the company. Also the manager has more power to offer compensation or to rectify the problem. An apology works wonders, especially if it is accompanied by a token to acknowledge the problem, such as a discount voucher against future orders.

423 REVIEW YOUR SERVICE CONTINUALLY.

Contact customers, or a cross section of customers, some time after delivery and check that they are happy with what they bought and with your service to them. You can do this by email or by telephone. This gives you feedback on your operation and also gives you another legitimate chance to sell something. Your customer may have ordered one of something to try it out – if they are happy, you may get a larger order immediately. If they have any problems, apologise and deal with them.

424 REMIND EVERYONE IN YOUR ORGANISATION THAT YOU ARE ONE COMPANY.

It is everyone's problem if a customer is unhappy. Never let one department or staff member criticise another; customers will not be reassured about a company that is warring with itself. Focus on beating your competitors, not your colleagues.

425 TREAT CUSTOMER COMPLAINTS AS AN OPPORTUNITY, NOT A PROBLEM.

As well as exposing specific problems that need to be fixed, customer complaints are a great opportunity to learn and improve. They should not be buried away and forgotten, but analysed. It's also good to share both positive and negative feedback with everyone in the organisation. If a staff member is mentioned by name, pass this on for praise but don't publish it in the case of criticism. This reminds everyone how important it is to keep customers happy – and provides a well-earned pat on the back when things go well.

CUSTOMER RELATIONS, REPEAT BUSINESS AND RECOMMENDATIONS

ENGAGE WITH CUSTOMERS

In the Internet age, old ways of doing business will no longer cut the mustard. There is a new power in customer's hands, and if you don't deliver the service that they expect, they want to tell the world. There are very few barriers to expressing strong opinions about companies online, and these opinions, positive or negative, can receive top search engine rankings, and pop up when people search for your brand. At the same time, customers can help each other and also broadcast how great you are. Understanding some of the dynamics of this world is important for success. Four ways that you can engage with your customers using these new technologies are forums, blogs, with customer feedback systems and with Social networks.

426 CONSIDER BLOGS, FORUMS AND FEEDBACK.

A blog is a series of small articles that you post regularly on your site. They tend to be very informal and could cover your products, company, experiences in business or even your hobby and social life. They will provide the most benefit if they relate to your business. A forum is a discussion board where customers can interact together and with your staff, discussing popular concerns and helping each other to solve problems. It's only worth running a forum if you have a large and engaged customer base running into the thousands, or traffic will be so low that it will give a negative message. A forum also requires a reasonable commitment of staff time in order to manage the forum and prevent it turning into a spammer's paradise. Remember also the section on how to get more from Social Networks.

427 REMEMBER THAT NOTHING PUTS PROSPECTS OFF LIKE TUMBLEWEED BLOWING IN THE WIND.

If you decide to publish a blog, host a forum or publish customer feedback, make sure there is a reasonable flow of new posts or information. If there isn't, it will actually detract from the business. Almost the worst mistake is to start a blog with great fanfare, then not post for months. If you haven't posted for two weeks, delete all mention of the blog from your site. Similarly, don't start a forum unless you have thousands of customers. The traffic won't be sufficient to sustain a conversation.

428 MAKE BLOGS WIDE RANGING.

Don't make your blogs straight sales pitches. No one wants to be pitched to, and the results will be the opposite of what you intend. Instead, talk around the subjects and demonstrate your expertise with interesting anecdotes and advice. The halo effect will inevitably increase your sales.

429 MANAGE YOUR FORUM.

It's hard to get a forum started and the minimum that you need is thousands of customers and a substantial number that are passionate about the area that you operate in. If you have a forum, you must be involved in managing it. In particular, any forum with a reasonable amount of traffic will attract spammers who paste all sorts of inappropriate content across the face of the screen. In short order the value of your forum will be destroyed and your customers will flee, never to return. To actively prevent this you must use the inbuilt forum protection measures and ruthlessly delete any violators. You also need to help with questions when answers are not forthcoming from other customers, and ban anyone who launches a campaign against you. Valid criticism is not and reasonable disagreements are not included in this.

430 USE INDEPENDENT FEEDBACK.

The advantage of asking your customers for feedback on your products and service is that this is something that pretty much every business can do, while forums are only applicable to large businesses and blogs require a talent for provocative writing. There are several benefits that come from displaying feedback from customers, and these are even better if the feedback is managed by a third party service. If feedback is held on a third party site with links to your site, this will provide search engine optimisation benefits. Independent feedback is more trusted and will glean a higher proportion of buyers giving feedback which will lead to a diverse range of opinions that come across as very credible. This will lead to a higher conversion rate, typically 10% or more than the same site without feedback. There is also an objective view of the company, which can be very helpful for the person managing things as they can get to hear how the land really lies.

431 LEARN FROM THE CRITICS.

While there are some negative people around who always see problems with everything, there is also rarely a disaster where somebody wasn't pointing out the problem in advance. The Bernie Maddoff fraud? The Securities and Exchange Commission in the US was tipped off years ago. Financial Crisis? It was all predicted by many people. For an example try searching for "Peter Schiff was right" on YouTube. He foresaw the whole pack of cards coming down and was laughed out of court for his pains. None of us like to be criticised, but the critics frequently hold the truth that we lack. It's a sad fact that there are some constant naysayers around, and they may have to be ignored. However, we dismiss all criticism on that basis at our peril. If that's us, our egos are probably getting in the way. If we want to be really successful in business, we need to be open to criticism, especially from our customers. As well as exposing specific problems that need to be fixed, customer complaints are a great opportunity to learn and improve. They should not be buried away and forgotten, but analysed. That way the negative becomes constructive, and we will improve performance as a result.

CUSTOMER RELATIONS, REPEAT BUSINESS AND RECOMMENDATIONS

TIPS TO HELP YOU STAY SANE

While business can be fun it's best to know that you will face some challenges. All of the points in this section are claimed to have happened for real, so thank you to all of the online merchants who contributed these tales of woe. This section is meant to provide some light relief, but also to prepare you, so when you face this sort of situation you can continue to behave totally professionally. Seriously, if you can't cope with this sort of situation, find another line of work.

432 BEWARE OF EMAIL INSANITY.

You get an email that asks: "Where is my order?" You check and check, and then learn that the customer actually bought from another site. Then there's the person who sends an email with a request, then follows up with an increasingly threatening tone because you've not responded in minutes. Finally there's the lady who sends an email with no subject line or message other than "Has my order been dispatched?" And of course, her email address doesn't match anything that you have.

433 WATCH OUT FOR THE UNREASONABLE.

An order is placed using a stolen credit card. The actual credit card holder calls up, explains that the charge was fraudulent, and you apologise and give them a full refund. A few weeks later you receive a chargeback for the same transaction even though it was refunded. Another person orders the same product twice, with the orders placed three days apart. However, the customer maintains that it is the merchant's fault. Yet another customer buys a custom-built product, then decides they are unhappy for no specific reason and wants to return it. When refused, they demand a refund from the credit card company.

434 NOT THE SHARPEST KNIFE IN THE DRAWER PREPARATION.

Look out for the customer who asks, "Send me your catalogue" even though you have stated you don't have one. Then there's the American customer who orders off a UK site, priced in pounds, then complains and issues a charge back because they weren't charged in dollars. Then there are people who agitate because you didn't deliver earlier than the time you have clearly stated on your web site. Again, you will find customers who live in a block of flats but don't bother mentioning the flat number. Finally there's the person who threatens you with legal action for non-delivery, only to find out that their secretary had taken the parcel and stored it away some two weeks earlier.

435 SWALLOW HARD.

Consumers using a credit card typically have a lot of power when there is a disagreement over their purchase. They can simply make a report to the credit card company and it is up to you to prove they are wrong or their payment will be charged back. It is also very possible for a disgruntled customer to blacken your name online and such negative feedback may show up first when potential customers search for your company name. As a result, when you confront the totally unreasonable it is best to make a tactical retreat. You can decide to stand up for what is "right", but that is usually the wrong business action. Best to settle, move on, and make sure you never accept another order from this customer. As compensation, some fraud checking services allow you to feedback on customers, and if they behave unreasonably several times they may have increasing difficulty in getting their orders accepted.

436 KEEP LISTENING.

Fortunately, while a few customers are totally unreasonable, probably 98% of difficult customers have good reason to behave as they do. Smart business people learn from their customers.

437 FIGHT BACK HARD.

There are a variety of things that merchants can do to fight back if that is actually what they choose to do and it is justified. Tactics include taking customers to the small claims court if you suffer an unjustified chargeback and warning them that you will report them to the police for fraud if they are behaving fraudulently (best to have details of their local police station and a local officer to quote if possible). You can also write a threatening but polite letter, warning them you will take court action, or that the account will be referred to a debt collection agency. If you have genuinely unique products you might even be able to get away with refusing cards and only accepting money transfers before dispatch. That way you won't be subject to the credit card company's rules.

438 LAUGH OUT LOUD!

This short section is designed to help you raise your tolerance levels – before you are called on to use it. Best to have a sense of humour at how strange humans can be and not take things personally.

TOP TIPS **439–442**

FINAL THOUGHTS

FINAL THOUGHTS

SOME FINAL TIPS TO REMEMBER

We don't want to miss anything out so here are some additional tips on a variety of topics.

439 WORK PAYS OFF.

There are a lot of tips in this book, and it would take a lot of effort to implement them all. But hard work has its reward. If you put the effort in, you will get the reward. My only warning is that prioritising your time, and ensuring that you finish one set of tasks before starting the next, is an additional discipline you need to make your hard work really pay off.

440 IF YOU CAN'T GET BIG, GET NICHE.

The web is huge, but you can be successful by being different. Maybe you can present a range of specialist products that is hard to find elsewhere. So narrow your niche and expertise down to a size where you are able to be better than the competition.

441 BE REALISTIC.

Not everything can be sold online. If you can't buy it by telephone, it probably won't sell over the net. Having said that, it is surprising just what does work and sells successfully online.

442 CHOOSE A SOLUTION THAT CAN GROW WITH YOUR BUSINESS.

Remember – you get what you pay for. Choose proven software with a good track record that is capable of handling your business growth. Make sure that the supplier is successful enough to still be around in a few years time.

THANK YOU FOR GETTING THIS FAR

I would like to acknowledge the invaluable information gleaned from publications such as Catalogue and E-Business Magazine and presentations and reports from the following organisations: The Catalog Exchange, IMRG and E-Consultancy. All of these organisations provide an invaluable service to the ecommerce industry and membership of at least one is recommended to any reader.

My thanks are also due to my colleagues Ben Dyer, Bruce Townsend and Tim Pritchard from SellerDeck who have each contributed chapters and have helped hugely in editing the text. I could not have completed this project without their helpful input, particularly in the fields of social networking, search engine optimisation and use of Google Analytics.

That's it! It just remains for me to wish you all success with your online venture. I hope that you join the ranks of those making a decent living from this source, or even become one of the elite making a genuine fortune.

ABOUT SELLERDECK

Since 1996, SellerDeck has been helping small and medium businesses trade online easily and at low cost. SellerDeck is a leading supplier of packaged ecommerce solutions for merchants, and ecommerce development software for web designers. The estimate of ecommerce orders taken through SellerDeck sites is over £11 billion and rising.

SellerDeck provides award-winning applications that include everything a small or medium business needs to build and manage their own online store. All products integrate every element of an online store into a single turnkey solution, from site design and maintenance through to processing of orders and printing of invoices. Site design can be customised from a range of design theme templates, and catalogue updates are easy to make. A built-in order processing facility includes support for phone and mail orders; flexible shipping and tax handling; back-ordering; stock monitoring; and reporting. SellerDeck integrates with all leading payment providers.

The SellerDeck range embraces options priced and capable of supporting businesses from small early stage businesses through to hundreds of thousands of orders and tens of millions of pounds per annum.

For more information and videos and demos of ecommerce, visit www.SellerDeck.co.uk.